Global Classics

What makes classics "global", and what does it mean to study the ancient world "globally"? How can the study of antiquity contribute to our understanding of pressing global issues? *Global Classics* addresses these questions by pursuing a transdisciplinary dialogue between classics and global studies.

Authoritative and engaging, this book provides the first field-wide synthesis of the recent global turn in classics as well as a comprehensive overview of an emerging field in ancient studies. Through focused readings of ancient sources and modern scholarship, the author introduces readers to three key paradigms that are essential to research and teaching in global antiquities: transborder, transhistorical, and transdisciplinary.

Global Classics will appeal to educators, students, and scholars interested in the application of globalization theories and paradigms in ancient studies, in globalizing their teaching and research, and in approaches to contemporary global issues through the study of the remote past.

Jacques A. Bromberg is Assistant Professor of Classics at the University of Pittsburgh (USA). His research covers ancient disciplinarity, the Socratic tradition, classical receptions in Latin America, and globalization studies. He is founding editor of the open-access journal *Global Antiquities*.

Routledge Focus on Classical Studies

This new series, part of the Routledge Focus short-form programme, provides a venue for the most up-to-date research in the field of Classical Studies. The series covers a range of topics, from focussed studies on specific texts, figures, or themes, to works on wider issues.

Prophets, Prophecy, and Oracles in the Roman Empire
Jewish, Christian, and Greco-Roman Cultures
Leslie Kelly

Theophrastus' *Characters*
A New Introduction
Sonia Pertsinidis

Gallus Reborn
A Study of the Diffusion and Reception of Works Ascribed to Gaius Cornelius Gallus
Paul White

Democracies and Republics Between Past and Future
From the Athenian Agora to e-Democracy, from the Roman Republic to Negative Power
Carlo Pelloso

Global Classics
Jacques A. Bromberg

For more information about this series, please visit: www.routledge.com/Routledge-Focus-on-Classical-Studies/book-series/FOCUSCLSS

Global Classics

Jacques A. Bromberg

LONDON AND NEW YORK

First published 2021
by Routledge
2 Park Square, Milton Park, Abingdon, Oxon OX14 4RN

and by Routledge
605 Third Avenue, New York, NY 10158

Routledge is an imprint of the Taylor & Francis Group, an informa business

© 2021 Jacques A. Bromberg

The right of Jacques A. Bromberg to be identified as author of this work has been asserted by him in accordance with sections 77 and 78 of the Copyright, Designs and Patents Act 1988.

All rights reserved. No part of this book may be reprinted or reproduced or utilised in any form or by any electronic, mechanical, or other means, now known or hereafter invented, including photocopying and recording, or in any information storage or retrieval system, without permission in writing from the publishers.

Trademark notice: Product or corporate names may be trademarks or registered trademarks, and are used only for identification and explanation without intent to infringe.

British Library Cataloguing-in-Publication Data
A catalogue record for this book is available from the British Library

Library of Congress Cataloging-in-Publication Data
A catalog record for this book has been requested

ISBN: 978-0-367-54926-8 (hbk)
ISBN: 978-0-367-55269-5 (pbk)
ISBN: 978-1-003-09265-0 (ebk)

Typeset in Times New Roman
by Apex CoVantage, LLC

Contents

Preface   vi

Introduction   1

What is global studies? 2
What is global classics? 6
Scope and outline of the book 12

1 Transborder   16

Locating the global in antiquity 17
Global and ecumenical in Polybius 26
Glocalization at Ai Khanoum 33
Conclusion 41

2 Transhistorical   49

Time and place 50
Tradition, reception, and beyond 61
Conclusion: multiple antiquities 71

3 Transdisciplinary   78

Holism, ecumenicism, and the global 79
Toward a critical global classics 88
Conclusion 98

Epilogue   102

Works cited   105
Index   122

Preface

This book is itself in many ways a preface to the broader project of "globalizing" the field of classics. It is written to introduce and model the methods that characterize the recent global turn in the study of the ancient world, to provide a field-wide synthesis of approaches to globalizations in antiquity, and to imagine some of the directions that the field might take from here. But as we will see, the concept of globalization is only one starting point for a greater transformation of classics that is already underway. My hope is that colleagues invested in this transformation will advance the dialogue, which this book enthusiastically advocates, between classics and global studies.

There are many friends and colleagues who made this project possible and, once it was underway, who made it better. I am especially grateful to the faculty and staff of the Global Studies Center (GSC) at the University of Pittsburgh for the Faculty Fellowship (2019–2020), during which the book was conceived and developed: Michael Goodhart, Veronica Dristas, Maja Konitzer, Elaine Linn, Roger Rouse, and Kat Lieder. When I began my collaborations with the GSC, I was amazed and delighted to discover that I had in fact been "doing" global studies for years without knowing it. My interests in ancient disciplinarity, classical receptions, and the intersections of literary genres share a discomfort with boundaries that global studies has helped me to think about and understand. Among the programs facilitated by the Faculty Fellowship were a yearlong lecture series, "Classics and the Global," and a graduate proseminar, "Global Issues through Classics," both of which enriched my thinking on questions of globalization and long-term sociocultural change. Guest lecturers in the series, Sailakshmi Ramgopal, Rebecca Futo Kennedy, Donna Zuckerberg, Kate Burmon, Micah Myers, Peter Meineck, and Naomi Campa, offered diverse and provocative perspectives on ancient connectivities. Thanks are likewise due to the proseminar's participants, Carolina Forgit-Knerr, Bryce Hambach, Eric Jordahl, Dafne Lastra Landa, Phillip Mendenhall, and Claire Ptaschinski,

Preface vii

for many lively and insightful discussions as well as for their patience and good spirits with a new course piloting an experimental curriculum. In my preparation for (and throughout) the fellowship year, support from the Department of Classics was essential. Mark Possanza (in every way the model for what a departmental chair should aspire to be) assisted in planning the seminar and championed it when it looked as though it might be under-enrolled. Among my colleagues here in Pittsburgh, I also thank Ed Floyd, Ellen Lee, Marcie Persyn, Carrie Sulosky Weaver, and Anne Weis for attending the public lectures, asking thoughtful questions, and promoting the year's events. A timely visit to Pennsylvania State University at the invitation of Eric Hayot permitted me to share an early version of the project with an erudite and imaginative audience.

The book is dedicated to my wife, Lisa, for her unwavering support as much as for her skill as interlocutor. The cliché that "none of this work would be possible without her" is more than usually true in this instance, since it was Lisa's work at the GSC that first put me in touch with its programs and opportunities. I hope that this book will, in some small way, be worthy of the many lessons and insights that she has given me.

Introduction

This book is about how our understanding of the ancient past and our relationships to it has changed during the most recent era of globalization. In addressing this question, this book investigates how classics and related disciplines have responded to the development of globalization studies, global studies, and related fields. It attempts to bring into conversation diverse contributors across various subfields, and to provoke further research and dialogue within classics and across disciplines, by outlining what "globalized" classics might look like. It is motivated by questions about what it means to study classics "globally," about the models and methods (traditional, prevailing, and forthcoming) for the global study of antiquity, and about the ethics of addressing contemporary global issues through classics. As an attempt to outline and define an academic subfield, including decades of trends across interrelated disciplines, the discussion at times is necessarily theoretical. Nevertheless, a thoroughgoing theoretical treatment is all the more desirable in the case of *Global Classics*, because both the "global" and the "classical" are contested concepts that fall outside of traditional disciplinary structures of specialized knowledge.

Popular characterizations associate both fields with the history and destiny of the so-called "West," whose influence has endured through time and across space and must therefore be inevitable or desirable or both. Conceptions of ancient Greece and Rome as the roots of "Western" civilization are in constant tension with specialized, historical facts and theories, most of which acknowledge that the "West" is a recent ideological construction. Meanwhile, popular views of globalization as the unstoppable march of "Western" ideas and values across the planet are at odds with definitions that understand globalization as a complex and multidirectional dynamic linking local, regional, national, and planetwide systems. The study of both globalization and the ancient Greco-Roman past is thus challenged by their problematic associations with the cultural imperialism and legacy of the "West" and by multiple competing attempts at self-definition. The fields of global studies and, the subject of this book, global classics have emerged to address these challenges by writing narratives that reveal the interconnectedness of human societies over time and by engaging colleagues and students across disciplines in discussions about the shared past and present. These narratives spring from the thesis that the study of nation-states cannot account for the social, economic, and political processes of an increasingly interconnected planet either today or in the past. Poverty, inequality, war, xenophobia, nationalism, migration, terrorism, and imperialism are major issues in today's world that are shaped both by their local contexts and by global processes. Replacement of approaches centered on nations with others rooted in globalization can offer paradigms by which to study our modern existence as well as the lived experience of antiquity.

What is global studies?

Global studies is an academic field dedicated to investigating globalization (its history, dimensions, dynamics, and effects). Since entering the popular discourse in the early 1990s, the term globalization has become evocative of many aspects of contemporary life: the integration of markets, the reach of communication and surveillance technologies, the erosion of local traditions and cultures by consumerism and corporate-capitalist logic, the threat of climate change, the spread of illness, and the movements of people across borders in response to these (and other) phenomena. It is not surprising that the term has generated significant debate and a sprawling academic literature across disciplines: how to define globalization, when it began, how it relates to what preceded it, and whether it is a good or a bad thing.

The most common definitions connect globalization with the growth of multinational corporations in the 1970s and the spread of transnational corporate capitalism, especially through the postcolonial, so-called "Third World." Globalization is perceived by many as an inevitable force, a "spectre," as it is often described, promoting Western values, products, and interests.[1] Both popular and scholarly books have compounded its reputation as a homogenizing process that privileges "Western" ways of living, working, and governing. This widespread account, however, is only one among a great diversity of theories about globalization and its origins, and scholars have proposed alternatives to the "West against the rest" that emphasize connectivity, mobility, and shared consciousness.[2] Here are some examples:

1 Globalization can thus be defined as the intensification of worldwide social relations which link distant localities in such a way that local happenings are shaped by events occurring miles away and vice-versa.
(Giddens 1990: 64)

2   Globalization as a concept refers both to the compression of the world and the intensification of consciousness of the world as a whole.
("Robertson" 1992: 8)

3   A social process in which the constraints of geography on social and cultural arrangements recede and in which people become increasingly aware that they are receding.
(Waters 1995: 3)

4   Globalization may be thought of as a process (or set of processes) which embodies a transformation in the spatial organization of social relations and transactions—assessed in terms of their extensity, intensity, velocity, and impact—generating transconnectional or interregional flows and networks of activity, interaction, and the exercise of power.
(Held, McGrew, Goldblatt, and Perraton 1999: 16)

5   A world of disjunctive flows [which] produce problems that manifest themselves in intensely local forms but have contexts that are anything but local.
(Appadurai 2000: 6)

6   Globalization is the imposition of the same system of exchange everywhere.
(Spivak 2003: 72)

7   Globalization refers to the expansion and intensification of social relations and consciousness across world-time and world-space. . . . Globalization is about growing worldwide interconnectivity.
(Steger 2017: 17)

These definitions emphasize similar features: increased interconnectivity through communication and trade, the compression of time and distance, and a shared sense of imagined transnational belonging. Nevertheless, the similarities break down upon closer inspection, with some treatments emphasizing transactional features (economic, financial, political, cultural), others the roles of human social consciousness, and a few attempting to combine the two. This spectrum of emphasis, rooted in distinct disciplinary approaches, reveals the multidimensional nature of globalizing processes.

Further disparities appear when the question turns to the origins and histories of globalization and, relatedly, whether these processes have shifted qualitatively over time or only in their intensity and in our awareness of them.[3] For some, the last 30 years mark a qualitative shift accelerated by international air travel and instant worldwide electronic communication.[4] A majority of scholars trace globalization to the period of transatlantic

4 *Introduction*

European reconnaissance and the establishment of trade routes and markets linking all of the inhabited continents.[5] Critiquing the inherent Eurocentrism of this view, others have argued for a longer history of interconnectedness, one that spans millennia and has expanded globalization history beyond Europe into Africa, Asia, and the Americas.[6] Because globalizing processes play out simultaneously and over time across many realms of experience, some have come to prefer thinking in terms of multiple globalizations. This proposition reflects a shift away from treating globalization as a single, homogenizing process and toward an approach reflecting a wide range of disciplinary perspectives.[7] As the editors of the journal *Globalizations* explain in the inaugural issue,

> by beginning from the premise that there are many globalizations we open the door to exploration of multiple processes and multiple interpretations and perspectives that may constitute many possible alternative globalizations, many possible paradigms.[8]

An illustration of this shift appears in Justin Jennings' *Globalizations and the Ancient World*, which attempted to distill definitional criteria for globalization in order to argue that multiple past globalizations have emerged during periods of long-distance connectivity and cultural change, leading to the creation of a "global culture".[9] Jennings defends case studies of three ancient globalizations in Mesopotamia, North America, and the Andes, which modeled his view that urbanization brought about the kinds of cultural change that deserve to be considered globalizing. But just as importantly, he makes a compelling case for premodern globalizations, in the plural.[10]

Because globalizing processes are multidimensional and unfold in different domains over time, sometimes simultaneously and other times asynchronously, this diversity of scopes, methods, and critical approaches is to be expected. Globalization studies, in fact, is perhaps best thought of in terms of this kaleidoscopic variety of disciplinary approaches, theories, methods, and data sets, extending far beyond the social sciences.[11] Nevertheless, global studies is more than studies of globalization. Programmatic accounts of the field have focused their attention on its deprioritizing of the nation, its broad, inclusive data set, its interdisciplinary orientation, its multicentrism, and its commitment to framing *and* addressing pressing global issues and risks. Global studies seeks to transcend "international" studies by including not only interactions between and among nations but also dimensions of interaction that transcend nations. The study of *international* migration, for instance, which focuses on the policies and experiences shaping the movement of peoples between nations, differs from the study of *global* migration, which includes these policies and experiences alongside structures and dynamics that transcend national boundaries. This wider scope offers a perspective that is global" by incorporating a larger, multidisciplinary data set. Jerry Bentley characterized this aspiration as addressing the need for comprehensive accounts of the global past that can model and frame historical analysis. Historicizing globalization is essential to creating meaningful and realistic accounts of the world, including transcultural connections, relationships, networks, interactions, and exchanges that humans have created since they first ventured outside of their communities over two million years ago.[12] Likewise, A. G. Hopkins has distinguished global history ("an attempt to bring order to world history by promoting comparative studies") from the history of globalization ("which attempts to assess the value of the social science literature on this subject for understanding the past").[13] In attempting to globalize imperial history by showing how modern empires were precursory agents of globalization, Hopkins' global history adopts a *longue durée* perspective, in line with large-scale, evolutionary, cultural narratives like Big History.[14]

While most studies of globalization take place within individual disciplines, global studies is transdisciplinary. Global processes are complex in nature, unfolding unevenly over time and leaving traces across many dimensions of lived experience. For this reason, a full appreciation of their global manifestations through time is only possible from a variety of disciplinary perspectives. Through the multidisciplinary exploration of issues that transcend nations and national history—for example, migration, race, colonization, enslavement, trade—global studies brings into focus something called, "the global." This imaginative, analytical category represents a reorientation away from the national, regional, and civilizational approaches that have characterized approaches to society, history, and culture. It also decenters Eurocentric/occidentalist histories in favor of a multicentric synthesis that views global issues from diverse perspectives. The need to globalize global studies by bringing scholars from diverse lifeways into the conversations shaping the field is central to its success. Recognizing the disjuncture between the knowledge of globalization and the globalization of knowledge, Appadurai has observed how globalizing processes paradoxically hinder the kinds of collaboration that would otherwise facilitate their analysis and understanding.[15] Though the field is still young—the first doctoral program in global studies at a major university, the University of California, Santa Barbara, is only six years old—some already see the danger of it evolving into a white men's club, privileging the interests, priorities, and perspectives of elite academics of the Global North.[16] By raising concerns that global studies has been perceived by colleagues in the Global South as a North American obsession, bordering on parochialism, such comments

6 *Introduction*

underscore the field's commitment to its redefinition from diverse, multicultural perspectives. For these reasons, the study of "globalization" is only one part of the academic synthesis of global studies. An understanding of the relationship between conceptions of globalization and the academic field remains a central question. Steger and Wahlrab's lively, introductory primer includes globalization as the first of four "pillars" (globalization, transdisciplinarity, space and time, and critical thinking) upon which they build their conceptual framework for the new field.[17]

Finally, global studies is problem-based in its approach to global questions and has strong interests in activism, advocacy, and policy making. Since globalization reflects an increasing sense of shared global coexistence and belonging, global studies capitalizes on this "global imaginary" to stimulate collaborative action on perceived global risks and threats: climate change, hunger, poverty, inequality, religious extremism and terrorism, enslavement, piracy, and cultural imperialism, among many others. These issues are difficult, if not impossible, to outline and comprehend by methods that are *not* global in their perspective and multidisciplinary in their approach. The global study of climate change, for instance, requires engagement not only with climate science, ecology, and agriculture but with theories of economic impact, development, urbanization, consumerism, technology, and sustainability; with histories of policy making and regulation at various levels (local, regional, national, and international); with philosophies of social and environmental justice; and with a multilingual and multicultural spectrum of rhetorics (denial, apocalypse, utopia) and poetics (ecocriticism, ecopoetry, cli-fi).[18] Complex processes and systems are also impossible to understand outside of deep social and cultural histories about people, power, and ideas. The multicentric, transdisciplinary, cross-cultural study of the interconnectedness of the world therefore has profound implications for the study of past societies; however, at the same time, our understanding of those interconnections, their origins, and their development draws from historical narratives with roots in antiquity. For this reason, a dialogue between global studies and classics is mutually reinforcing.

What is global classics?

This book outlines and models a direction in classical studies that seeks perspectives on global issues through multicentric, comparative, and interdisciplinary approaches to ancient culture and history. *Global Classics* describes methods of classical research and scholarship that are dedicated to the study of globalizing processes, systems, and structures in and since antiquity and to the study of the globalization of classics itself as a discipline. It is predicated on three core suppositions. The first is that global issues are not only transnational but transhistorical. Much of the modern, global arrangement of peoples, power, ideas, and resources has come into being through multifaceted processes spanning millennia, with deep roots in the various, global antiquities of human civilization. My second supposition is that, because of the transdisciplinary character of the field, classics is ideally positioned to add in important ways to discussions of global issues, which are too complex to approach from a single, disciplinary perspective. Not only can classics provide a great deal of empirical data to the growing database of global history, but as a transdisciplinary field itself, classics can offer decades of experience with the advantages and risks of transdisciplinarity. Third, the field of classics itself is at a crossroads, faced with questions of relevance and problems of access and inclusivity that threaten its existence. *Global Classics* offers strategies for addressing these anxieties within the profession by broadening the field's horizons, responding to mounting institutional pressures, and engaging new colleagues, students, and audiences in stimulating conversations about past and present.

I deploy the term classics advisedly as a designator for the academic field that includes Greek and Latin philology, ancient history, Mediterranean archaeology, philosophy, reception studies, and related subdisciplines. But like globalization, classics is a contested term. Just as globalization is often thought to describe the spread of "Western" values across the planet, classics has often been imagined as a vehicle for propagating "Western" values through time. The Latin word (*classicus*) from which "classics" derives was used in antiquity to designate the cultural sphere of the upper class, and the field has deep roots in elite, cosmopolitan discourse and European cultural imperialism.[19] Greek and Latin sources occupy a privileged position in the canons of literature, politics, art, and architecture, though some have critiqued the omnipresence of imperialism, tyranny, enslavement, inequality, and violence in the ancient world.[20] They are foundational texts in many modern academic disciplines, including several that are deeply invested in the study of globalization, such as anthropology, sociology, and political science.[21] Because of their prominence in the traditional education of European, colonial elites, the Greek and Roman classics sit uneasily alongside other ancient cultural histories with which they might be compared and studied.

On account of the cultural capital they possess, Greek and Roman sources, ideas, and artifacts have been appropriated and weaponized in the culture wars of the past half-century, even as their place at the center of the canon has been challenged and their role in education diminished.[22] Few would deny the role of classics and of classicists in promoting occidentalist, Eurocentric, and ethnonationalist agendas in the past. Examples and lessons from antiquity are still routinely marshaled in promoting orientalist/

occidentalist ideologies that imagine a never-ending "clash of civilizations" between a civilized "West" and a barbaric "East." In recent decades, these narratives have been invoked to promote and justify military and economic interventions around the world.[23] This inherited occidentalism is one of many problems facing classics today. Other historical and philosophical fantasies about independent, yeoman farmers, soldier-citizens, amateur athletes, happy slaves, and avuncular slave owners have whitewashed crueler realities, and from this fabricated and sanitized antiquity, more insidious fictions have grown. The modern aestheticization of whiteness by apologists for the mass-enslavement of Africans and by their successors in white supremacist movements fed on ancient climate theories of race and on fantasies that imagined the ancient Greco-Roman world as a place of white bodies in white buildings.[24] In its ugliest manifestations, this appropriation of antiquity has made ancient Greece and Rome into ancestral homelands of a fictitious "white" race and has played a role in motivating unspeakable acts of hate.[25] The rejection of these views by scholars as misappropriations or misreadings does not mean that they are totally baseless and invented. On the contrary, hate groups are often able to marshal ancient texts effectively not through ignorant misreading, but because ancient texts often *do* in fact express sentiments of xenophobia, misogyny, and contempt for cultural "others."[26] As an accessory to the westernization thesis of globalization, therefore, classics has a long and painful history of exclusion at all levels with which the field is only beginning to come to terms.[27] *Global Classics* cannot promise to rescue the field from this history or to spare it from whatever difficult reckonings await. This little book can only aspire to outline a few avenues toward a globalized, decolonized, and more inclusive discipline.

For over two decades—indeed, ever since the idea of globalization first became a subject of investigation—classicists, ancient historians, and archaeologists have discussed how to respond to this global moment: some have focused their attention on whether and how the ancient Greek and Roman world was itself globalized, others have focused on the roles that antiquity and perceptions of antiquity have played in shaping global issues and events, and still others have focused on how to globalize the modern profession. As others have noted, the attempt to define what classics means in the age of globalization is not only an academic exercise but a strategic undertaking. Classical histories offer valuable metaphorical perspectives on the contemporary world, and the globalization of premodern histories may make them more interesting to a wider audience.[28] Over the past decade, the aim of educating "global citizens" has become a common aspiration for twenty-first-century universities. This aspiration runs so close to cosmopolitanism that modern departments of classics must craft their missions

Introduction 9

carefully in order not to fall prey to temptations of occidentalism, elitism, and exclusivity. Nevertheless, the task of imagining how courses of study in antiquity can contribute to the global aspirations of modern colleges and universities is critical to the health of the field in the new academic environment. So how can the paradigms offered by global studies be useful to the study of the ancient world, and reciprocally, how can the study of antiquity help us to study global issues today?

Most scholars would recognize that globalization is more than a popular trend in social science research. A growing number of classical scholars have taken the concept of globalization itself seriously as an interpretive tool. This book attempts to bring together their efforts, exploring and advancing the variety of globalizing trends across classics and offering a programmatic description of a new area of specialization that advances these trends. Its central thesis is that classics and global studies are ideal interlocutors. *Global Classics* adopts the theories, methods, and interpretive frames of global studies to write deep historical narratives of globalization as well as focused microhistories that reveal globalizing processes through time. Thus, the narratives of global classics are both globalizing and global, both heuristic and descriptive. By promoting holistic, transdisciplinary approaches to antiquity, the field advances ongoing efforts to decenter ancient studies away from its traditional fixation on urban cultural centers and the elite experience of antiquity. By adopting a transnational, globalizing model for the study of ancient words, it also adds to existing frameworks for writing historical narratives that emphasize cross-border fluidity and interconnectedness rather than fixity and separation.

Classical scholars have been engaging with global questions for decades, reframing the discipline's geographical and temporal borders through comparative, interdisciplinary research. Horden and Purcell's monumental volume, *The Corrupting Sea*, reflected decades of dissatisfaction with a paradigm that understood social and cultural identities as fixed, static, and regionally bounded. Instead, the authors proposed to study the Mediterranean as part of an interlinked antiquity characterized by transregional cultural and economic flows.[29] The new paradigm coincided with the development of a new Mediterraneanism, which adopted frameworks of world-system theory, network theory, globalization theory, and global history in order to free ancient history from its isolation and Eurocentrism.[30] In the intervening years, scholars have extended these frameworks to write histories of colonization, migration, and mobility, to describe complex dynamics of trade and material culture, and to pursue the comparative study of empires.[31] The essays on Roman history, economics, and archaeology collected by Martin Pitts and John Miguel Versluys demonstrate how globalization theory can and should be used to understand the Roman world.[32]

10 *Introduction*

Many prominent scholars have studied the active dialogue between cultural insiders and outsiders in the shaping of Mediterranean and Near Eastern societies and identities.[33] Others have ventured beyond literary texts by urban, male elites and embraced comparative methodologies that put diverse ancient literatures in touch with one another.[34] Interest in writing by and about people on the various margins of the ancient world has grown in ways that have shifted attention away from the urban centers, upper classes, and "golden ages" of cultural production.[35]

A globalizing impulse has also illuminated sources that fall outside the usual periods of ancient literary studies and has shifted attention beyond the ancient world to the postclassical afterlifes of ancient texts, objects, and ideas. The studies of the classical tradition and of classical receptions have capitalized on this decentering movement and established themselves as essential methodologies with significant potential to globalize the field.[36] A complementary approach to these two methodologies has emerged in the form of theories of world literature, which are focused on the ways that literary works circulate beyond their time and place of origin, either in their original languages or in translations.[37] These examples reveal that scholars in classics have long appreciated the potential of globalization studies to offer a window on the ancient past and, conversely for the ancient world to shine a light on the globalizing present. They also demonstrate a diversity of method and focus that mirrors the disciplinary variety of global studies, fostering an increased capacity to investigate, understand, and explain complex systems and processes.

All of this activity across the field—in ancient history, Mediterranean archaeology, and classical studies—suggests that a paradigm shift is underway, leading us toward new ways of thinking about forms of interconnectivity both within antiquity and between antiquity and today. This book is not the first work of scholarship to call this shift in orientation global classics. At the 2019 annual meeting of the Society for Classical Studies, society president Joseph Farrell put this project on center stage. In both the presidential panel and his presidential address, Farrell focused on the discipline's dimensions, provoking questions about how the ancient and modern worlds have been partitioned and whether traditional divisions remain viable.[38] This book draws from and aspires to respond in a valuable way to Farrell's provocations. Though the work that has been done bringing theories of globalization into classical scholarship surely constitutes a "global turn" in the field, significant gaps and pitfalls remain.

Despite the enthusiasm with which some scholars have welcomed the analytical methods of the social sciences, only a few have actually engaged with globalization per se.[39] Due to the omnipresence of the word in public debates, many early influential accounts employ a narrowly circumscribed understanding of globalization, popularized in the Anglo-American media, that frames globalizing processes as unidirectional, inevitable, and homogenizing.[40] This view of globalization has led others to adopt the language of contemporary, transnational, market capitalism in searching for ancient history's economic and cultural winners and losers, a preoccupation that risks reinforcing the cultural essentialism and bounded societal rigidity that global cultural studies aims to transcend. The presumption that the "global" overrides the "local" is at odds with the view of globalization as unfolding through an interplay of global and local. This multilevel approach to globalization, characteristic of global studies, is the product of an engagement with disciplines (e.g., anthropology and sociology) that operate at different social scales, another reason why multidisciplinarity is an essential feature of the field. It is also a sign of the field's commitment to supplementing the dominant top-down macro narrative of globalization ("globalization from above") with accounts of "globalization from below" that view processes of global social change from the perspectives of those who "do the legwork of globalization."[41]

Other quarters of the discipline also reflect this top-down orientation. Two of the field's allegedly most globalizing movements, the study of classical receptions and the study of the classical tradition, remain dominated by studies of elite texts, poetry, and drama most of all. This fixation can be explained in the case of the classical tradition by its focus on the dissemination through education of ancient texts and ideas. But the field of classical receptions is not immune to this privileging of elite perspectives, texts, and orientations. These trends suggest that scholars of ancient literary and cultural studies have internationalized, but not globalized their methodologies. This distinction may look like wordplay, but it is far from trivial. It describes the persistent tendency to approach ancient texts and objects using influential, cognitive frameworks of modernity, which cannot be relied on to provide an accurate account of premodern social and cultural change. These frameworks include the system of territorial nation-states and the schemes of periodization, by which scholars have traditionally divided the expanses of space and time. Scholars have not yet disentangled classics from national borders in a satisfying way in that investigations of the ancient world are often subject to the conceptual limitations of a state-centered perspective that has come to be known as "methodological nationalism."[42] Globalization of these methodologies in ways that de-emphasize the unbroken, diachronic chain of elite texts; the hegemonic, value-laden language of heritage or debt; and the cognitive frameworks of territorially bounded, sovereign nations requires new frameworks of investigation ("methodological globalism") that emphasize global interconnectedness.

12 *Introduction*

While it is exciting that scholars are making connections between ancient and modern cultural histories and using theories of globalization to study processes of social change in antiquity, it is regrettable that developments are taking place in relative isolation from one another. The study of the ancient Mediterranean is hyperspecialized in ways that discourage the comparative, cross-disciplinary, multiperiod study of processes and trends.[43] A large intradisciplinary gap separates social, political, military, and economic historians from scholars of literature, philosophy, religion, cultural, and intellectual histories. An even greater gulf divides them from scholars of classical traditions and receptions. These gaps suggest that even scholars enthusiastically pursuing projects on ancient globalization have yet to assimilate the useful differences between studies of globalization and global studies and to draw on the strengths of classics as a transdisciplinary field. The field's recent multidisciplinary "global turn" reflects the need for a new specialization that combines the study of cultural change *across space* (through mobility, connectivity, and decentering) with the study of cultural change *over time* (through traditions, receptions, recoveries, and reinventions of the past). Globalizing classics means developing methods of synthesis and argument that bring issues in ancient literary studies into dialogue with issues in ancient history and archaeology, but it also means imagining how the discipline can grow to help us understand processes that transcend the boundaries (between regions, cultures, periods, and fields of specialized knowledge) that have traditionally defined it. This book is organized as an investigation and exploration of these three dimensions of the new global classics: space, time, and discipline. The study of transcultural flows through time unites these trends of current scholarship to offer a kaleidoscopic perspective on the ancient world as a global, interconnected, enduring, and more inclusive antiquity.

Scope and outline of the book

Global Classics makes its case for a dialogue between classics and global studies by illustrating how global ways of thinking and teaching can enrich the study of the ancient world and how classics can offer perspectives that illuminate pressing global issues. The complementary modes of thinking and teaching that constitute the new global approach to classics are the core organizing principles of this book. By presenting detailed theoretical formulations alongside focused readings of diverse ancient materials, *Global Classics* aims not only to explain the new heuristic but also to demonstrate some of its potential interpretive value. These examples illustrate that the structures and arrangements of past and present are mutually constitutive through processes that are best understood as globalizing. The book

Introduction 13

is structured around three core trans- concepts that inform this dialogue: transborder, transhistorical, and transdisciplinary. All three challenge the field's traditional boundaries by exploring ancient sources and approaches that transgress them, and in so doing they present perspectives, analogies, and contrasts that are useful in discussions of current global issues.

My hope is to offer a conceptual framework that supports the theoretical, empirical, interpretive, and pedagogical work of professional researchers and educators. The chapters address individually how transborder, transhistorical, and transdisciplinary paradigms are framed within the discourse of global studies, where they intersect with current trends in classical scholarship, and how they enrich our understanding of antiquity. Chapter 1 addresses the theme of globalization in the ancient world, differentiating among key terms such as "international," "transnational," and "global." I address objections to the use of the term global to describe aspects of antiquity and identify structures and arrangements that facilitated the interconnectedness of the local, regional, and superregional. Theorizing globalization's cross-border dynamics mobilizes a core principle of global studies to rethink the traditional borders that have defined the study of ancient Greece and Rome. The global does not override the local, but the interaction between global and local is a recurring theme in global research. This dynamic, which has sometimes been described as "glocalization," is central to the perception and expression of shared social consciousness, a defining feature of globalization. I introduce evidence from literary, historiographical, and archaeological sources that model global and glocal approaches to antiquity.

Chapter 2 builds on this discussion of globality to present a theoretical framework for transhistoricism, mapping and modeling transhistorical thinking as conceptually analogous to transborder/global thinking. Transhistorical thinking encourages readers of ancient sources to challenge borders between traditional historical periods and to consider alternative periodizations that capture the continuities and disruptions of human life in and since antiquity. I connect this construction with a recurring motif in globalization research, namely, the compression of space and time. This explanation facilitates an analogy between transnational and transhistorical thinking: in the same way that transnational thinking helps us to consider processes and structures that cross geographical boundaries, transhistorical thinking helps us to identify and study processes and structures that transcend perceived periodic boundaries. In this way, transhistorical thinking offers a critique of postmodernism as a state of alienation from the past and offers alternative temporalities, including ones that emphasize continuity over disruption.

In Chapter 3, the argument shifts from the contents of the field of classics to its institutionalized framework. The field's global turn reflects a perception that the traditional divisions of specialized knowledge in classics cannot answer questions about long-term human interconnectedness. It also signals that a reorientation of the field toward new, problem-oriented modes of inquiry is underway, one which requires transdisciplinary collaboration and investigation. Transdisciplinarity is a core principle of global studies enshrined in many programmatic accounts of the field.[44] While vital to the study of global issues, which is too complex to approach from the perspective of a single academic field, transdisciplinarity is an unappreciated feature of classics. Classics, like global studies, integrates a variety of disciplinary approaches and insights into its conceptual framework; both fields seek ways to supplant presentist, Eurocentric/occidentalist epistemologies shaped by the national imaginaries of the eighteenth and nineteenth centuries.

Finally, it is important to appreciate that global studies has developed to address specific problems in social well-being resulting from the transnational connections and disruptions of globalization. The field has a strong interest in public policy, activism, advocacy, and community engagement. Theoretical reflection, even when grounded in rigorous empirical analysis of diverse data, is therefore insufficient. In answer to this imperative, globalizing classics means applying the interpretive work of classical scholarship, historical analysis, and archaeological investigation to yield useful insights and practical solutions to real-world problems. This task is especially important if we hope to bring classics into dialogue with transdisciplinary fields like global studies, as *Global Classics* aims to do. Creative, global research design and pedagogy combine sources, media, and methodologies to recover marginalized viewpoints and engage diverse audiences in dialogue about global issues, informed by detailed comparative study of global pasts.

Notes

1 The word "spectre" or "specter" appears in discussions of globalization by Dunne (1999), Appadurai (2000: 2), Holton (2011: 77 and *passim*), Jennings (2011: 32), Pitts and Versluys (2015a: 10), and Steger (2017: 1).
2 Appadurai 1990: 295; Robertson 1995: 26–34; Waters 1995: 6, 136; Holton 2011: 2–3; Steger 2017: 1–2.
3 See useful surveys in Waters 1995; Holton 2011; Pitts and Versluys 2015a: 12 and 15–18; Nederveen Pieterse 2015: 225–228; Steger and Wahlrab 2017.
4 Harvey 1989: 293; Castells 1996; Cairncross 1997; Steger and Wahlrab 2017: 3–7.
5 Robertson 1992: 49–58; Waters 1995: 4–5; Holton 2011: 47–8; Dunne 1999; Flynn and Giráldez 2006; Nederveen Pieterse 1995: 47, table 3.1.
6 Abu-Lughod 1989, 1993; Frank and Gills 1993; Ekholm and Friedman 1993; Wilkinson 1993; Jennings 2011; Nederveen Pieterse 2015.
7 Nederveen Pieterse 1995: 45–6; Gills and Thompson 2006: 4.
8 Gills 2004: 1.
9 Jennings 2011: 21.

Introduction 15

10 For claims to the contrary, see Stearns 2010: 5.
11 Nederveen Pieterse 1995: 45, 2013: 505–508.
12 Bentley 2004: 77–78.
13 Hopkins 2010: 24–25.
14 Hopkins 2010; Spier 2015.
15 Appadurai 2000: 4.
16 Darian-Smith 2015: 166.
17 Steger and Wahlrab 2017: 18–19 and ch.1.
18 Johns-Putra 2016.
19 Aulus Gellius (*Attic Nights* 19.8.15) famously used the term to distinguish a "high class" (*classicus*) author from a "low class" (*proletarius*); cf. Plautus, *Miles* 752. Martindale 2007: 310–311; Ziolkowski 2007: 17; Schein 2008: 75–77.
20 Shumate 2006; Hingley 2015: 36–37.
21 Wolf 1982 on anthropology; Inglis and Robertson 2004 on sociology; Ober 2006 on political science.
22 duBois 2001; Adler 2016; Bloxham 2018.
23 E.g. Huntington 1996; Allison 2017.
24 Kendi 2016: 17–21, 113–114.
25 Many recent manifestations documented online by *PHAROS* (http://pages.vassar.edu/pharos/ accessed 10/20/20).
26 Zuckerberg 2018.
27 Padilla-Peralta 2019; Rankine 2019; Seo 2019; Bostick 2020.
28 Morris 2003: 40.
29 Horden and Purcell 2000.
30 Morris 2003; Malkin ed. 2005; Hingley 2005; Hodos 2006, 2010b; Vlassopoulos 2007; Hitchner 2008; Müller 2016; Jiménez 2010. Discussion to follow in Chapter 1.
31 Sweetman 2007; Malkin 2011; Vasunia 2011.
32 Pitts and Versluys 2015b.
33 Kuhrt and Sherwin-White eds. 1987; Hartog 1988; E. Hall 1989; Miller 1997; Moyer 2011; Haubold 2013.
34 Vasunia 2001; Haubold 2013.
35 Newlands 2002; Dougherty and Kurke 2003; Bosher ed. 2012; Pogorzelski 2016; Stewart 2017; Kennedy 2014; Wijma 2014; Vasunia 2001; Kasimis 2018.
36 For the classical tradition, see Highet 1949; Bolgar 1973 [1954]; Kallendorf 2007; and Silk, Gildenhard, and Barrow 2014. For classical receptions see Hardwick 2003; and Hardwick and Stray eds. 2008; Butler ed. 2016.
37 Doniger 1999; Damrosch 2003; Beecroft 2010, 2015; Denecke 2014.
38 Farrell 2019.
39 E.g. Hingley 2005; Naerebout 2006–2007; Sweetman 2007; Hitchner 2008; Müller 2016. The edited volumes by Pitts and Versluys (2015b) and Hodos ed. (2017a) are a significant advance in this regard.
40 Morris 2003: 33 and 41–2; Malkin 2011.
41 Nederveen Pieterse (2013: 509) lists among these bottom-up globalizers, "seafarers and dockworkers, poor migrants, social movements, and grassroots initiatives." Darian-Smith and McCarty 2017: 37–39 and *passim*.
42 Holton 2011: 16–17; Pitts and Versluys 2015a: 7–8; Steger 2017: 7–13; Darian-Smith and McCarty 2017: 154–158.
43 Cherry 2004: 235–236; Knapp and van Dommelen 2010: 3–4.
44 For example, Steger and Wahlrab 2017; Darian-Smith and McCarty 2017.

1 Transborder

One of the goals of this book is to reframe the study of antiquity as a global enterprise. This reframing involves remapping the field's contours, centers, margins, and peripheries and reassessing sources from a globalized perspective. Ancient texts, sites, and artifacts make up a complex data set that reflects shifting relationships and interactions between distinct localities and reveals a range of attitudes and conceptualizations relating those localities to larger regional and cultural units. The combination of classical scholarship with theories of globalization offers a powerful interpretive framework through which to study these connections. This chapter models a transborder approach to antiquity that combines critical orientations within classical scholarship with interpretive frameworks of global studies to show how this combination of methods can generate new knowledge.

The chapter's sections promote approaches that recognize the fluidity of ancient boundaries as a complement to approaches that privilege bounded states. I focus on transborder processes in order to offer a model for decentering Greco-Roman antiquity, and I present two case studies that demonstrate evidence for perceptions of shared supraregional consciousness grounded in distinct localities. The first case study involves Polybius, whose universal history globalization scholars and social theorists view as one of the earliest texts to attempt to understand the "whole inhabited world" as a single interconnected place. The second case study presents evidence of the coproductive dynamics of local and global from the transcultural site of Ai Khanoum in Afghanistan at the border of the ancient world or, one might say, in between ancient worlds. These forms of inquiry encourage scholars open to interdisciplinarity and collaboration to globalize classics outside of the ancient Mediterranean. Sites on what has often been considered the periphery of Greece and Rome, where ancient cultures met and interacted, allow us to imagine and pursue alternative, hybrid antiquities. The comparative study of global antiquities is one potentially transformative model for the field of classics.

Locating the global in antiquity

Global studies seeks new panoramas on the world and its history by applying conceptual pressure to borders of all kinds. The most familiar borders, and the subject of a great deal of social science research, are territorial boundaries that constitute the modern system of sovereign states. Studies of globalization track the processes, flows, systems, and networks that transcend these boundaries and reveal a thickening interconnectedness between people in different parts of the world. For this reason, "decentering" or "destabilizing the center" is often cited as one of the field's core concepts, and it is the chief focus of this chapter.[1] Almost every academic discipline has its own conceptualization of and approach to globalization: sociologists are interested in transnational social connectivities and the emergence of a global society; economists are interested in the worldwide integration of supply chains and markets and the internationalization and regulation of global finance; and historians are interested in making connections between systems and tracing processes through time.[2] Some inquiries focus on the objective dynamics of globalization and its role in creating or disrupting transactional relations between people and polities, while others attend to its subjective processes, especially the perception of growing worldwide interdependence and shared social consciousness.[3] Global studies may be understood as an open-ended, multidisciplinary synthesis of these and other approaches to globalization and its effects.

So what about classics? Can we even talk about globalization in antiquity? The search for ancient globalization requires differentiation between terms that are often treated as synonymous, but that are in fact distinct. The terms "multinational" and "international," both describing processes or arrangements across the boundaries of two or more countries, assume the reality of fixed boundaries between nations and take these bounded entities as fundamental units of analysis. By contrast, "transnational" and "global" refer to processes and arrangements that transcend the limits of bounded polities, operate over long distances, and connect people in different parts of complex, transborder social networks. One example might be the transnational societies of migrants who remain socially, religiously, economically, and in other ways simultaneously connected with their societies of origin.[4] Diaspora and border studies are transnational methodologies that investigate systems and processes at and across the margins of sovereign nations.[5] In the context of ancient studies, treaties, and political confederacies, *synoecism* and citizenship grants are examples of transpolitical structures.[6] Other examples include the multinodal, intellectual network of itinerant poets and philosophers in the seventh, sixth, and fifth centuries BCE; the development and perseverance of a diasporic Messenian identity among the enslaved helot population of ancient Laconia; and the interconnected, maritime and commercial networks and hybrid material cultures of the Hellenic colonies in southern Italy and Sicily, their metropolises, and their neighbors.

Both transnational and global thus denote processes, interactions, and arrangements that transcend the limits of a single polity, especially those that operate and connect people across regions. Kearney defines global processes as "largely decentered from specific national territories and take place in a global space," in contrast to the more limited purview of transnationalism, which describes processes that are "anchored in and transcend one or more nation-states."[7] Even if they do not operate in every part of the planet, processes are sometimes described as global because compounds of nation(al) are only appropriate once a division into sovereign territorial states has become widespread if not ubiquitous. One might object that neither transnational nor global is appropriate to describe premodern periods that antedate the modern system of nation-states and whose cultures and societies operated only in parts of the globe. It was not until the 1970s—with the disappearance of most formal colonial systems—that most of the world was organized according to the current system of bordered, territorial nations represented by sovereign states. This perception informed early theories of globalization, which sought its origins in the spread of multinational corporations in the 1970s and 1980s and the competition for markets, resources, and development opportunities in the postcolonial, "Third World". Embracing David Harvey's postmodern characterization of the 1970s and 1980s as "another fierce round in that annihilation of space through time that has always lain at the center of capitalism's dynamic," Cairncross credited modern developments in transportation and communication with bringing about the "death of distance".[8] The Spanish sociologist Manuel Castells charted the development of a global "network society" through advances in communication technologies.[9] The emergence of a specifically twentieth-century "global imaginary" is a common trope in discussions of globalization.[10]

Most histories of globalization, however, begin in the sixteenth century CE. The "early modern" period contextualizes globalization within Marxist histories, centered on the growth of the world market and the global division of labor. This chronology has become so influential that the year 1500 CE has been described as a "Great Wall" separating modernity from antiquity, and indeed, something approaching a consensus exists that globalization is only five or six hundred years old.[11] Some scholars insist on a strict use of globalization to denote only processes that encompass or affect the entire planet. Flynn and Giráldez argue that true globalization emerged in 1571 when the foundation of Manilla allowed direct trade between Asia

Transborder   19

and the Americas: "Prior to that year, the world market was not yet fully coherent or complete; after that year it was."[12] Waters also identifies the sixteenth century as the moment when it becomes possible to talk about the global: "globalization could not begin until that time because it was only the Copernican revolution that could convince humanity that it inhabited a globe."[13] Influential scholars who locate the origins of globalization in this period include Immanuel Wallerstein, whose world-systems theory is an important precursor in the Marxist tradition to globalization studies; Roland Robertson, who posited a premodern, "germinal" phase of globalization in Europe in the fifteenth century, though in his account globalization did not "take off" until the nineteenth century; and Anthony Giddens, who saw globalization as a consequence of modernity.[14]

Inspired by Braudel's vision of the early modern Mediterranean as a "world-economy," Wallerstein viewed globalization as a basic element of a multicultural, cross-border economic system beginning in the sixteenth century.[15] Distinguishing the world-economy (a multicentric system of unequal, competing polities) from the premodern arrangement of "world-empires" (defined by a single, controlling polity), Wallerstein saw in globalization the triumph of the capitalist logic of accumulation. His theory explained the interconnections among populations spread over great distances through arrangements in which a single political system dominates (world-empires) or in which a variety of political systems compete (worldeconomies). He considered the European world-economy that developed out of the Middle Ages a world-system "not because it encompasse[d] the whole world, but because it [was] larger than any juridically-defined political unit."[16] Though Wallerstein allowed for premodern world-systems, he argued that the modern world-system was unique and located the origins of globalization in the year 1500 CE.[17] Because of its utility in historicizing globalization, world-systems theory has been widely influential, refined, and critiqued. Giddens complained of world-systems theory's heavy concentration on economic influences, preferring to view globalization within the broader experience of modernity, which he called "inherently globalizing."[18] Accordingly, the world capitalist economy was only one of four dimensions of globalization that have emerged since the sixteenth century, alongside the nation-state system, the world military order, and the international division of labor.

The early modern period is enshrined in histories of globalization due in part to the efforts of A. G. Hopkins to delineate the field of global history. Hopkins attempted to reinvigorate the study of modern empires by presenting a new developmental model that combined the subdisciplines of historical investigation (urban, imperial, political, economic, colonial, etc.). Hopkins defined globalization in terms of the imperial centers and their satellites, which facilitated new forms of belonging. Initially, globalization was reflected in a cosmopolitanism that reinforced the imperial power's own sense of nationhood. Over time, new regional and supraregional alliances came to serve as safeguards against westernization, and in a final phase, new economic unions further eroded the industrial state's claims to national sovereignty.[19] Hopkins' influential collection of essays, *Globalization in World History*, attempted to trace this early modern history of globalization, challenging accounts that treated history as a linear process and globalization as a very recent phenomenon (starting in the 1980s) with one that outlined the origins and sequences of globalization since the sixteenth century.[20] His work inspired other historians, including classical historians, to search for globalization and globalizing processes in premodern history.[21]

In response to these theories and histories, some argued that Marxist narratives, like world-systems or dependency theory, are rooted in Eurocentric histories of capital and labor and struggle to explain premodern societies. Early modern and modernist narratives also center on a European experience of modernity, privileging the urban imperial centers, while downplaying their complicity in enslavement and colonialism and ignoring the roles of diverse localities in globalization's dynamics.[22] As a consequence of these emphases and omissions, presentism and occidentalism, as well as a focus on male cultural elites, pervade studies of globalization that trace its origins to sixteenth-century Europe, limiting their scope both chronologically and geographically. Paul Gilroy has linked these narratives with a pernicious form of racism that he calls "foundational ethnocentrism," which glosses over or downplays modernity's ties to colonialism and enslavement. Nederveen Peiterse has remarked that linking globalization with modernity is "a theory of Westernization by another name."[23] Pushing against Wallerstein's periodization of the world-system, Janet Abu-Lughod argued for a "thirteenth-century world system" that linked eight city-centered regions between Central Asia and the Indian Ocean from 1250 to 1350 CE.[24] She identified a precursor to Wallerstein's sixteenth-century world-system and made room for the study of further premodern globalizations.[25] The effort to "provincialize" European history by subordinating it to alternative, cultural histories is part of the greater postcolonial project challenging Eurocentric accounts of Western culture and its origins.[26] Writing from newly independent African nations, Cheikh Anta Diop (Senegal), Théophile Obenga (Congo), and Yosef ben-Jochannan (Ethiopia) argued that Greek civilization derived from African cultures, especially Egypt, whose language and culture they claimed were African in origin and influenced by other ancient African empires.[27] Their arguments anticipated the interventions by, notably, Martin Bernal and Samir Amin, whose alternative cultural histories shifted attention, respectively, to North Africa and the eastern Mediterranean.[28]

Seeing even these globalizing developments as too limited, Andre Gunder Frank and Barry Gills proposed "a wider world-historic humanocentric alternative to Eurocentrism."[29] Their collection of essays, *The World System: Five Hundred Years or Five Thousand?*, extended the chronology of world-systems, exploring interconnections and integrating regions that Wallerstein and others had marginalized. David Wilkinson's essay, for instance, synthesized cross-civilizational research of fourteen worldsystems, stretching back over five millennia, into a series of episodes of a previously unknown entity in Egypt and Mesopotamia, which he names "Central civilization:" "today there exists on the earth only one civilization, a single global civilization . . . created in the Middle East during the second millennium BC by an atypical encounter between two pre-existing civilizations."[30] Wallerstein and Samir Amin rebut this critique by emphasizing differences between precapitalist societies and the modern world-capitalist system. Though globalization itself is hardly mentioned, the volume dramatizes the rich debate of the early 1990s about the history of worldwide economic interconnectedness.

Classical scholars have responded to these developments in world-systems theory, globalization theory, network theory, and global history in a variety of ways. Over the past three decades, a movement to liberate antiquity from Athenocentrism, Laconicentrism, Romanocentrism, and the like has swept across the field. Classicists, ancient historians, and archaeologists have all contributed to this project by investigating the ways in which boundaries, centers, and peripheries have been drawn, theorized, and used to construct knowledge about local, regional, and pancultural identities. This decentralizing movement has taken many forms. One significant effort to decenter ancient texts involves confronting long-held beliefs and assumptions about links between the literary production of classical Athens and its democratic form of self-government. In contrast to the widespread view that "only Athens" could have developed and promoted dramatic genres, scholars of Greek drama have challenged its perceived Athenocentrism and argued for tragedy as a Panhellenic phenomenon.[31] In a similar vein, studies of imperial Latin literature have challenged its perceived Romanocentrism, by demonstrating the ways poetic and historiographical narratives by Ovid, Silius Italicus, Martial, Statius, and Tacitus craft worldviews that shift Rome and the emperor away from the center of the action.[32]

In drawing attention away from urban centers, ancient literary studies have supplemented the dominant narratives (male, free, elite, citizen) with other complex identities and literary subjectivities. Edith Hall's *Inventing the Barbarian* is an influential example of an approach to Greek literature (tragedy, in this case), informed by social scientific frameworks, that examined the construction of Athenian self-image through an imagined "other."[33]

22 Transborder

Studies of the cultural appropriations from Egypt, Persia, India, and other ancient societies have revealed the multifaceted dynamics through which communities crafted and revised their senses of self.[34] By reflecting on how tragic, historiographical, and philosophical texts illuminate Egypt's unique place in the Greek imagination, Vasunia's *Gift of the Nile* demonstrates how Athenian literature crafts and deploys a "myth of Egypt" to address a variety of concerns and anxieties.[35] His attempt also to contrast the Athenian idea of Egypt with the ancient Egyptians' own sense of self reflects the influence of postcolonial and cultural studies, an approach that has aided in the development of a dialogic model to cross-cultural interaction in antiquity.[36] Work on ancient multiculturalism has come also to examine the ancient subcultures that are revealed through closer attention to material objects (e.g., vases, inscriptions) and nonelite texts (e.g., fables).[37] Research on people on the margins of society (foreigners, women, immigrants, brigands, slaves, workers, and the poor) has spread appreciation of the importance to ancient literary studies of understanding dynamics of race, class, gender, ethnicity, and legal status and has produced enriching, new readings of familiar texts.[38] The same decentralizing impulse that has drawn attention to the experience of social outsiders in studies of ancient texts has driven the growth of specializations that focus on the texts and materials of daily life in antiquity. It has expanded the use of noncanonical sources (inscriptions and papyri) to advance and substantiate complex, historical arguments about cultural trends.[39]

The most sustained engagements with theories of globalization have come from ancient history and archaeology, areas of the field already in close dialogue with the social sciences. One of the most significant developments of the past half-century in ancient Mediterranean studies has been the change in our understanding of ancient societies and cultures as fluid, rather than fixed and regionally bounded. How social, ethnic, and cultural identities are produced through migration, colonization, trade, war, and other forms of transcultural interaction has been a central question since the social scientific studies of ethnicity by Frederik Barth in the 1960s.[40] Barth argued that that cultural identities are "not primordial and fixed, but emerge and change in diverse circumstances: socio-political, historical, economic, contextual and—in the case of the Mediterranean's seas and mountainous islands—geographical."[41] In the ensuing decades, theories of political economy, core-periphery, and world-systems inspired new reading of social interactions and transformations in the ancient Mediterranean. Following Wallerstein, some scholars adapted a core-periphery model of social change, which emphasized forms of connectedness between local communities and the centers of power.[42] These models adopted a logic of acculturation that was especially obvious in debates about "Romanization," where the contrast between "becoming Roman" and "remaining native" dictated the movements of goods and people.[43] The dissatisfaction with the rigidity of this dichotomy drove the search for a new paradigm.

I can still recall the ripples of excitement swelling from the appearance of Horden and Purcell's ambitious and pivotal volume, *The Corrupting Sea*, on the shelves of our campus bookstore, and the exhilaration and admiration that it produced among my cohort of graduate students in classical studies and ancient history. The first multiperiod, pan-Mediterranean study since Braudel was, in the familiar words of one reviewer, an act of *"chutzpah,"* a project that would "take a generation of historians to digest and implement."[44] The authors sought to supplement Braudel's view of the ancient Mediterranean as a stage for the great events of history with a Mediterranean that functioned as a dynamic, interactive network of transregional, cultural, and transactional flows. Their model viewed Mediterranean cultural unity as a process resulting from the interaction of long-range and intermediate forces on a complex network of microregions. Both Greek and Roman historians acknowledged the potential of this new approach and produced new readings of ancient Mediterranean history that replaced the static and regionally bounded structures of the old model with interconnectedness and fluidity.[45] Although Horden and Purcell did not allude to the concept of globalization, scholars drawing from their work began using globalization theory to supplement traditional accounts of cultural transformation and write histories of cultural, political, and economic interconnectedness in antiquity. Ian Morris praised the volume as signaling a paradigm shift in ancient studies away from a model based on static cells and rigid structures to one based on fluidity and connectivity. Recognizing the value in pursuing ancient analogies to contemporary globalizing processes, he branded their equivalents in antiquity "Mediterraneanization."[46] Building on Horden and Purcell's effort to connect ancient history with the history of the greater Mediterranean and Near Eastern world, Greek historians have turned to globalization theories in hopes of finding an entirely new heuristic.

Irad Malkin's application of network theory to the interconnectivity of Greek communities in the archaic period is characteristic of the new "Mediterraneanism" that emerged.[47] The transborder paradigm acknowledged that the ancient Greek world had no dominant, cultural center where it developed and from which it spread. The norms and identities among the Greek states resulted from a vast, transpolitical network that was by nature decentered. Even over long distances, however, a cultural uniformity was apparent in every part of the Greek-speaking world. From the Black Sea to the coast of Spain to the Cyrenaica, a traveler would encounter uniformity in urban planning, architectural forms, religious practice, and language. Borrowing both from Castells and from Soja the postmodern idea of "shrinkage," Malkin turned to network theory to explain this homogeneity. His claim was, paradoxically, that the Greek world shrank as it grew, becoming more interconnected through divergence. This world was characterized by a system of hundreds of small, sovereign polities connected by a vast maritime, commercial network. Over the course of the archaic period, this decentralized network became homogenized, transforming between 750 and 500 BCE from a "many to many" network of Greeks, Phoenicians, and Etruscans to one characterized by homogenized subareas of activity (commerce, traffic, settlement) resembling modern "zones of influence."[48]

Critics of this alleged homogeneity, however, have pointed to the diversity within the greater cultural unity. One of the objectives of Kostas Vlassopoulos' polemic in *Unthinking the Polis* is pursuing "new units of analysis and new forms of historical narrative, which will enable us to study and portray the multiple histories of various groups of peoples, instead of the homogenizing and subjugating national narrative."[49] The book offers a multiscalar spatial analysis of Greek polises, tracking the structure of relationships between communities, their territories, and networks, between communities and their regions, and between communities and a world-system. Vlassopoulos' alternative narrative of Greek history proposes to escape the methodological nationalism of the polis by embracing the diversity of ancient evidence available through archaeological research. Compared with our extant historical sources written by the elite and focused on the urban centers, archaeological investigation has uncovered a wider and more inclusive body of evidence, including information unavailable from written texts: patterns of settlement, the arrangements of domestic space, and rituals of death and mourning. The attempt to write historical accounts that draw on this body of comparative, diachronic research, while reflecting the diverse circumstances, perspectives, and temporalities of lived experience, constitutes a new agenda for Greek historical studies.[50] Vlassopoulos builds on this foundation by mapping the diversity of interactions between Greeks and non-Greeks across four "parallel worlds:" networks involving the movement of people, goods, ideas, and technologies throughout and beyond the Mediterranean; the creation of self-organized, politically independent Greek communities in non-Greek lands; the world of Panhellenism that, in the absence of a single cultural center, fostered a sense of unity through a shared cultural heritage in literature, myth, religion, and art; and finally, the rise and competition of powerful empires, which not only directed the course of world-changing events through war, conquest, and diplomacy but also mobilized populations and resources in ways that shaped Hellenic history. In the space created by these processes emerged "a world of shared symbols and meanings" that, far from hastening the disappearance of local cultural identities, provided the means of Hellenic cultural expression in diverse contexts.[51] The mutually reinforcing dynamic between local and global, in which local communities and cultures draw from a shared world of meanings, is known as "glocalization,"[52]

Not all historians have embraced globalization as a means of understanding ancient history, and even enthusiastic advocates warn that it should only be used as a heuristic (not a descriptive) tool.[53] Despite the attraction of a globalizing model to explain the growth of Roman hegemony, its acceptance and application by Roman historians have been tentative and sparse.[54] Among the first to engage with the concept extensively was Richard Hingley, who used it as an interpretive tool by which to criticize the problematic idea of romanization in accounts of the spread of Roman cultural identity.[55] Hingley invoked the problematics of globalization as an analogy by which to mount this critique, using the example of globalization to demonstrate how histories of the Roman past continue to be written using the model of the present.[56] From this perspective, the research agendas in Roman archaeology and social history evolved as attempts to address contemporary political and economic concerns, without sufficient attention to the way accounts of the ancient past perpetuate forms of colonial knowledge. One of Hingley's salutary interventions is his reminder of the limits of modern analogies, which (like globalization, mediterraneanization, and romanization theories) can conceal forms of colonial knowledge and imperial agendas. Naerebout critiqued Hingley's use of the problematic and contested concept of globalization to describe the premodern world; but the critique failed to appreciate Hingley's use of globalization theory not to replace the paradigm of romanization, but rather to demonstrate the analogy's limitations.[57] Bruce Hitchner compares Roman globalization with the British Empire, using the term globalization to capture complex but recurring processes of human social change, of which the Roman Empire is only one example. Hitchner locates the "key transformative act" in the Romans' replacement of the fragmented system of individual polities with "a new interdependent system of non-sovereign territorial entities," but he concludes that his analogy invites a reconsideration of the way historians have ordered and conceptualized social change through time.[58] Whereas Naerebout critiques the problematic nature of the word globalization itself, both Hingley and Hitchner attribute globalization's value for Roman studies to its "fecundity and complexity" or "contested nature."[59] In response to objections that globalization can and should only be used to describe phenomena that are planetary in scope, Hitchner remarks that globalizing processes are matters more of relative perception than geographical scale. This characterization is surely accurate for several reasons. Globalization describes the growth over time of shared social consciousness and senses of belonging as well as the spread of transborder processes and relations that make those forms of perceived belonging possible. Approaches to ancient history informed by globalization studies therefore integrate evidence from local, provincial, regional, and global scales.

In the past few years, theories of globalization have been accepted and applied, not without caution and reservations, to the study of many realms of ancient life as they played out over time and across the ancient world. These debates remain alive and flourishing across many subfields of ancient studies, including in the study of ancient religion, mobility and connectivity, the study of the ancient economy, and studies of material culture and identity.[60] The case studies that follow in this chapter explore these features of globalization in the ancient world, undertaking first a brief account of Polybius' globalizing discourse and second a study of local-global dynamics in the Greco-Bactrian outpost of Ai Khanoum. These examples illustrate the relevance and utility of paradigms drawn from globalization studies in the study of antiquity.

Global and ecumenical in Polybius

In decentering antiquity, scholars have pursued a vision of a world characterized by flows, processes, and interactions between communities not regionally bounded but interconnected. This orientation contrasts with the one adopted in the political philosophies of Plato and Aristotle, whose texts make the city-state, the polis, the central feature of human social and political life. Plato's political philosophy in *Republic* and *Laws* places the polis at the center of discussions of justice and the ethics of government. The analysis in *Republic* involves a deliberate reframing of the inquiry about justice from the level of the individual to the level of the polis (368e8–369a3). Socrates' supposition is that justice will be easier to find and understand on the larger scale of the city, and so the discussion shifts in scale and focus. Aristotle advanced the view in *Politics* that the polis reflects the end-goal and truest natural instantiation of human social organization (1252b27–1253a1) and that a person who is "without a polis" (ὁ ἄπολις, 1253a3) is either less than or more than human (i.e., either a beast or a god). This privileging of the polis as the fundamental unit of analysis in human society reflects an outlook resulting from centuries of interstate rivalry and warfare. Plato was born (*ca.* 427 BCE) four or five years into the Peloponnesian War between Athens and Sparta; Aristotle died around the same time as Alexander the Great (*ca.* 323 BCE), having witnessed Alexander's conquest, destruction, and unification of the Hellenic cities. Reflecting on the diminished state of the city after Alexander, Aristotle argued for "self-rule" (αὐτάρκεια), as reflected in the polis, as the natural outcome of the evolution of all human social organization (*Pol.* 1252b29).[61]

These formulations privileging the polis have exerted tremendous influence on the history of social thought.[62] Inglis and Robertson see the polis-centered orientation of Plato and Aristotle as analogous to modern approaches to social organization that emphasize the nation or society, concepts understood to be fixed and endogenous. Replacement of these bounded concepts with ones in line with the concerns of globalization requires the development of new analytical categories and modes of thinking that reflect a more interconnected world. Inglis and Robertson argue that Hellenistic historians, especially Polybius, deserve recognition for their pursuit of analytical categories that permit the study of the whole inhabited world (*ecumene*).[63] The argument outlines a shift in the sensibilities of Greek historians in response to a regional hellenization that brought about an economic and political weakening of the individual polis. The conquest of the Greek communities by Alexander and his successors, and then later by the Romans in the second century BCE, accelerated and intensified the interconnectedness of the Mediterranean. Historical reflection shifted focus from interstate rivalries to transregional processes operating across the whole (perceived) inhabited world. In contrast to the narrowly focused chauvinism against barbarians of Herodotus and the annalistic, state-centric history of Thucydides, historians developed the genre of universal history committed to analyzing the affairs of the known world as part of a single, organic whole. Described by ancient authors as attempts "to write the affairs of the whole [world] [τὰ καθόλου γράφειν]" (Polybius 5.33.2) or to record "affairs common to all people [κοινὰς πράξεις]" (Diodorus Siculus 1.4.6), universal history aimed to give a structured and coherent account of events on a world scale.

It is generally acknowledged that the first author of a "universal history" was Ephorus from the city of Cyme on the Aeolic coast of Asia Minor, who lived in the second half of the fourth century BCE.[64] We know almost nothing of his life, and his writings (including a number of treatises in addition to thirty books of *Histories*) survive only in fragments. Because of Ephorus' division of his narrative into separate treatments of the Greek and non-Greek worlds, he is said to have been a student of Isocrates, an early advocate of Panhellenism.[65] As the first to undertake a universal history, Ephorus struggled with the question of organization, ultimately deciding to arrange his history into books covering human affairs "by type" (κατὰ γένος), a phrase that has caused much consternation, but is believed to mean "by geographical area."[66] The first three books dealt with the histories of the individual Greek cities, and ancient writers praised Ephorus' treatment of "their foundations, kinships, migrations, and founding figures."[67] Accordingly, Ephorus' method of organization may have provided a model for later universal historians (including Diodorus Siculus himself, as well as Appian,

Pomponius Trogus, and Posidonius) who may also have arranged their works geographically.[68] Out of dissatisfaction with Ephorus' long-term perspective, however, which arranged the knowledge of three-quarters of a millennium into separate historical accounts of Greek cities, social theorists have turned to Polybius.

Though Polybius seems to have thought highly of Ephorus, his history differed significantly in its focus on a particular moment in time when the history of the world appeared to be coalescing into a united whole.[69] In contrast to Ephorus' attempt to give a comprehensive historical account of the past, Polybius' history was universal in addressing a subject of pressing importance to the inhabitants of the entire ecumene at a global present: the fifty-three years (between 220 and 167 BCE, later extended to 145 BCE) that it took the Romans to conquer "nearly the entire known world" (σχεδὸν ἅπαντα τὰ κατὰ τὴν οἰκουμένην, 1.1.5). In describing the scope and aims of his work, Polybius reveals his perception of a shrinking, interconnected world and critiques historians for writing histories that focus on individual cities. The comprehensive perspective he offers is "impossible to perceive from the work of those writing partial histories [κατὰ μέρος]" (1.4.6). Polybius describes the events shaping his time as "resembling a living organism [οἱονεὶ σωματοειδῆ], insofar as the affairs of Italy and Libya are interwoven [συμπλέκεσθαι] with those of Asia and Greece, and the trajectory of everything leading to a single outcome [πρὸς ἓν ... τέλος]" (1.3.4).[70] This teleology is one of the unique features of Polybius' work, as he himself claims:

> the distinguishing feature of my treatment, and the great wonder of our times, is the fact that fortune has caused nearly all the affairs of the inhabited world [ἅπαντα τὰ τῆς οἰκουμένης πράγματα] to slope in a single direction, and compelled [them] to be inclined towards one and the same end.
>
> (1.4.1)

Alonso-Núñez identifies Polybius' concept of interweaving as the closest analogy to globalization from the ancient world.[71]

Modern social theorists have found the ecumenical analytic of universal history a useful framework for understanding globalization, in that it seeks to investigate (and at the same time is made possible by) conditions of increasing interconnectedness and shared sociopolitical consciousness.[72] The conquest of the ecumene by the Romans brought about a condition of widespread interconnectedness, and the genre of universal history was developed in response to these globalizing conditions.[73] This narrative is attractive to theorists and historians of globalization for obvious reasons. Polybius offers a snapshot of a globalizing age that appears analogous to our own: this period is characterized by a contest between two superpowers (Rome and Carthage) in which the defeat of one resulted in the political, cultural, and economic hegemony of the other; the process of conquest and the establishment of hegemony is characterized as a swift, recent development, taking place in less than half a century; and these events fostered a perception of widespread historical interconnectedness and shared social consciousness, as reflected in the production of universal histories themselves. Furthermore, Polybius appears to have shared with histories of globalization the belief that transregional interconnectedness was the recent product of his age. This attitude is revealed in Polybius' prologue when he contrasts the world affairs of previous epochs with his own. Before his time, he claims, the affairs of the ecumene happened "kind of randomly" (ὡσανεὶ σποράδας), "since each event was separate from others in terms of its course, its outcome, and its location" (1.3.3). The period characterized by this condition of separateness and regional historical isolation came to an end, in Polybius' estimation, when the Romans destroyed the Hellenistic dynasty of the Antigonid monarchs, who had ruled in Macedonia for over a century.[74] Writing from Rome in the aftermath, Polybius conceived his project as documenting not only how events in all parts of the inhabited world came together into a series of causally linked interconnections, but also what systems and processes allowed the Romans of his day to achieve something "that never before can be found to have happened" (1.1.5–1.1.6). The analogy with modern histories of globalization is ready-made: the globalizing (equal to first hellenizing and then romanizing) of Polybius' ecumene shifted into a higher gear during and in the centuries following the expedition of Alexander between 333 and 323 BCE and accelerated again during the period of Roman conquest that he narrated.

Several core assumptions make this analogy possible. One is the association of the polis only with certain periods of Greek history, such that its independent history comes sharply to an end in the fourth century BCE. Another is the supposition that the interactions and perceived interconnectedness between the Hellenic communities and, say, the ancient Near East, are products of the Hellenistic period. Both of these assumptions are questionable; some objections have already been mentioned, others will emerge shortly and (with regard to the problems of periodization) in the next chapter. Without a doubt, many aspects of interconnectedness have roots in the globalizations of still earlier periods: the Hellenic colonizing diaspora, the institutionalization of theoric networks and Panhellenic festivals, the writing of historiographical and geographical accounts, the transregional market for objects and labor, and the campaigns of Alexander. Explanations of the polis that focus on phenomena such as its autonomy, forms of self-governance, and civic identity formation are likely to miss the diverse, daily social and economic phenomena that constituted the lived experience of the community. "Instead of viewing the polis (in the sense of a community of citizens), or democracy, as the teleological and 'classical' outcome of the evolution of Greek political life," counters Vlassopoulos, "we should rather study how a variety of processes and activities coalesced into the formation of Greek polities and democracies."[75]

The idea that the polis loses relevance in the minds or daily lives of Hellenic communities after Alexander and the Romans is also overstated, as are claims that Polybius abandoned the cognitive framework of the polis in narrating his history. Polybius adopts a city-centered analytic in many places. In an interesting passage from the preface of Book 9 (9.1.4), he describes three "genres" in historical writing, which include "the genealogical type," the "sort about colonies and foundations and kinship (just as is related by Ephorus)," and a third "political [type] [τὸν δὲ πολιτικὸν] concerning the affairs of tribes (or provinces) and cities and rulers." He then claims that his entire work (τὴν ὅλην τάξιν, 9.1.5) belongs to the third category, which as Walbank noted, includes "all forms of state."[76] His description of the origins and evolution of the Achaean league in Book 2 (2.41) and his brief history of Elean neutrality in Book 4 (4.73–4.74) are instances where local microhistories (perhaps like those by Ephorus) inform his global account.[77] I use the word global deliberately here to recall the difference between Ephorus' and Polybius' "universal" histories. While Ephorus appears to have conceived of world history in terms that separated the history of Hellenes and of non-Hellenes (perhaps reflecting the Panhellenic idealism of Isocrates), Polybius focuses on the continuity and interconnectedness of events and the systems and processes that impacted them by organizing his history around a particular topic: the swift rise of Roman hegemony.[78] This fundamental difference between Ephorus' and Polybius' conceptions of universal history is captured in Craig Benjamin's distinction between world history and universal history:

> where world history attempts to provide an inclusive and broad ranging survey of events, universal history emphasizes the continuity and connections between those events by organizing them around a particular theme, or a handful of thematic frameworks, as a means of contextualizing and making sense of the events themselves, and of connecting these various "parts" together into a more organic and unified narrative.[79]

Compared to Ephorus' narrative, which covered over seven centuries (from *ca.* 1069 to 341–340 BCE), Polybius' narrative is at times strikingly granular: "all that befell the Romans and Carthaginians," he explains, "transpired on account of a single man and a single lifetime, I mean of course Hannibal" (9.22.1). This interest in the lives of individual actors in his drama parallels his view of the persons and events of his day as interconnected parts of "a corporate whole" (σωματοειδής, 1.3.4). While Ephorus separated the histories of Hellenic and non-Hellenic states in accordance with his organizational principles (κατὰ γένος), Polybius joined local political microhistories into a larger narrative in ways that justify his claim that the global affairs of his day are increasingly "interwoven" (συμπλέκεσθαί, 1.3.4).

The enduring relevance of the polis as a frame of reference is reflected in Polybius' use of spatial metaphors drawn from the familiar arrangement and architecture of Hellenic cities. In Book 3, for instance, Polybius describes how the Carthaginian position on the plain of Capua between tall mountains and the sea turns the space "as if into a theater" (3.91.10); in Book 6 he compares the arrangement of streets in a Roman military camp to a city (6.31.10). Katherine Clarke has observed Polybius' frequent invocation of the spatial arrangement of an acropolis to enhance his readers' ability to imagine scenes and landscapes (3.54.2, 5.8.6, 5.21.5).[80] Polybius justifies this practice by acknowledging that readers unfamiliar with these places may find his narrative "unruly and dull;" he therefore promises "always to connect and correlate unknown places with ones that are familiar and well-known" (5.21.5). In a similar vein, Diodorus Siculus comments in his preface that universal historians write "the affairs common to all people of the inhabited world [τὰς κοινὰς τῆς οἰκουμένης πράξεις] as if recording a single account of an individual city [καθάπερ μιᾶς πόλεως ἀναγράψαντες ἕνα λόγον]" (1.1.3). Appeals to the microcosm of the polis within the global narrative reflect the enduring importance of the polis as a frame of reference, even as these authors claim the whole inhabited world (*oikoumene*) as their subject.

Assumptions about interconnectedness in antiquity reflect an aversion to *longue durée* histories of globalization that is typical of globalization studies. Related to this attitude is the universal perception that globalizing processes, particularly those associated with technological advances, are always reaching their highest point in the period during which one lives. Polybius experienced the age of growing Roman hegemony as the "single culmination" (ἓν . . . τέλος, 1.3.4) of history, as every part of the inhabited world became linked. Describing his shrinking world, he explains how, "In our day, on account of Alexander's empire in Asia and Rome's domination of the rest, almost everywhere can be reached by sailing or marching" (3.59.3). His modern world had bigger ships than ever before (1.63.8) and, thanks to the establishment of peace in 146 BCE, had experienced "such progress in the arts and sciences [τὰς ἐμπειρίας καὶ τέχνας] in our day that scholars are able to master every event as it occurs in a way that is, so to speak, scientific [ὡς ἂν εἰ μεθοδικῶς]" (9.2.5).

These critiques should not detract from the value of the parallel that social theorists draw between Polybius' ecumenical orientation to world affairs and modern studies of globalization. On the contrary, his emphasis not only on the growing interconnectedness of places and peoples but on the structures and processes that facilitated it reinforces the similarities. The half-century of Roman expansion that Polybius witnessed and recounted transformed the ecumene in new ways still, widening its borders through military force and surveying, mapping, apportioning, and registering its lands. The arduous work of measuring and breaking up conquered territory can be construed as an appropriative act of romanization, one of many exertions of soft power through which the Roman hegemony brought about gradual, but lasting social change.[81] Harder to measure, but certainly no less real, was the degree to which the processes set in motion by the events of Polybius' narrative impacted forms of social identity. Elite dining culture reveals how transregional groups can become spearheads of globality, since aristocratic banquets and convivial culture have left a clear trail of similar objects and compatible social practices across space, from Palmyra to Spain.[82]

The Roman hegemony, which Polybius saw as the end of history, set in motion a series of social transformations such that 300 years later, around the year 144 CE, the Greek panegyrist Aelius Aristides could offer the following praise of Rome:

> You have brought about that saying of Homer, "the Earth was common to all," by your action, by measuring out the whole inhabited world [πᾶσαν τὴν οἰκουμένην], yoking rivers with all kinds of bridges and cleaving mountains to be land fit for carriages, filling deserts with posting stations, and pacifying everything with your way of life and your order.
>
> *Encomium of Rome*, 101[83]

Aristides' exuberant quote about the Roman ecumene reveals an awareness of a shrinking world. Written no doubt to flatter a Roman audience at the height of Roman power, the passage, and its surrounding context, extolled the virtues of regional integration under Roman imperial rule:

> No longer is it necessary to write a geographical description of the earth [περιήγησιν γῆς] . . . since you have flung open the doors of the whole inhabited world [ἁπάσας τῆς οἰκουμένης] . . . and created a common, public bond of marriage, arranging the whole inhabited world [ἅπασαν τὴν οἰκουμένην] as if it were a single family.

(102)

Though remarkable for its clarity and unique in its exuberance, his expression of globality under the Romans reflects on century-long processes that constitute the Roman globalizing project.

Glocalization at Ai Khanoum

A recurring theme in globalization studies involves the idea that globalizing processes are reflected in the interaction between local and global. Although one could perhaps imagine that many such processes have limits that might be measured on a planetary scale, few participants (if any) in these processes perceive them in that way. On the contrary, while some scholars view globalization as a homogenizing force and lament the destruction of forms and expression of local culture and identity, others see globalizing processes as rebuilding, enhancing, and even producing forms of locality through expressions of difference. These narratives reflect a powerful dynamic linking the local to the global, for which theorists have coined the term "glocalization."[84]

Appadurai characterizes the central problem of global interactions today as "the tension between cultural homogenization and cultural heterogenization."[85] Readers of Polybius' account could easily conclude that globalization chiefly involves large-scale processes of broad social transformation. Polybius' insistence that the Roman hegemony represented the end-goal of history (1.3.4, 1.4.1) and his descriptions of the shrinking of the globe are characteristic of an unquestioned tendency to think of globalization primarily in terms of large-scale phenomena. Such an impression of globalizing processes under the Romans would support not only the romanization thesis of cultural and social change but also the homogenization thesis of globalization, as characterized in many popular modern accounts. Marjorie Ferguson critiques the idea of cultural homogeneity as one of globalization's myths:

> Either this myth presumes that it is possible to argue the existence of a global cultural economy that ignores the counter pull of localism and the rich traditions of variance, or it assumes, wrongly, that cultural identities are contained within political borders or are conferred on a transhistorical world society basis by an ethic of consumption (or exploitation).[86]

Ferguson, and other critics of this myth, interpret the concept of cultural homogenization as referring to the triumph of the global over the local, two sociocultural constructions often taken as in tension with or opposition to one another. The mythologizing narratives that embrace this view of globalization treat globalizing processes as fundamentally in tension, even in competition with local cultures and identities. This view of globalization as involving large-scale, homogenizing processes is reflected in many studies of the new Mediterraneanism.[87]

A pithy example of this dichotomy between homogenization and heterogenization is Benjamin Barber's article "Jihad vs. McWorld," which presents a dystopian vision of a political future characterized by two irreconcilable dynamics: one centrifugal, heterogenous, and tribal and the other centripetal, homogenous, and global. In Barber's view, globalization, which operates transnationally and transculturally, is in competition with "forces of global breakdown, national dissolution, and centrifugal corruption."[88] Roland Robertson critiques Barber's argument for its reduction of a complex dynamic to a straightforward opposition between extremes. "There is no good reason," he explains, "other than recently established convention in some quarters, to define globalization largely in terms of homogenization."[89] Robertson argues that no definition of the global that excludes the local makes sense: the two are mutually constitutive. If globalization is to be defined as the compression of the world, then this shrinking involves the production and interconnection of localities. Robertson objects to the claim that prior to now most humans possessed stable identities in homogenous locales by critiquing the emphasis of nationalist ideologies on cultural homogeneity and reflecting on the forms of polyethnicity that were once common.[90] The homogenization thesis of globalization ignores the ways that local expressions of identity are produced. While narratives that support this thesis emphasize *top-down* social transformation on a world scale, the study of individual localities across the developing ecumene reveals a complex dynamic of *bottom-up* identity formation. The glocalizing approach modeled in this section presents an account that is sustained by the mutually constitutive relationships between local, regional, pancultural, and multicultural entities.

Glocalization can take various forms, reflecting diverse relationships between local and global. Local communities can adopt the practice of a foreign culture entirely or modify it in some way to suit their needs and priorities. They can mix cultural styles, creating hybrid forms of text, object, and building that fuse together local and foreign features, or juxtapose these features in ways that do not attempt to intermingle but signal their difference. At times, localities can even craft new glocalized forms out of globalized cultural practices that speak in different ways to community members of different cultural backgrounds. Vlassopoulos has explored these varieties of glocalization in antiquity by studying cultural practices in ancient Etruria, Caria, and Lycia.[91] The architectural, archaeological, and literary remains from the colonial city of Ai Khanoum in Hellenistic Bactria provide a range of evidence for glocalizing practices from a site on the edges of the Hellenic world or, to put it in a more relevant way, at the center in between ancient worlds.

The ancient kingdom of Bactria lies north of the Hindu Kush in the region around the Amu Dar'ya (the Oxus River in antiquity), a landlocked, mountainous desert thousands of miles from Athens (closer to Qin China, in fact) and totally unlike anything to be found in the Mediterranean.[92] In the middle of the sixth century BCE, the Persian king Cyrus added the territory to his Achaemenid Empire that ruled for over two centuries from the Gandhara to the Aegean. After defeating the Achaemenid armies at the Battle of Gaugamela, Alexander and his army marched through this landscape between 330 and 325 BCE, conquering Sogdiana, Bactria, Arachosia, and parts of the Indus valley. As part of his effort to control and stabilize the frontier, Alexander founded Alexandria Arachosia (perhaps modern Kandahar, Afghanistan) in 330 BCE, and the following year, he founded Alexandria Eschate ("Alexandria at the Edge," modern Khujand, in Tajikistan) at the easternmost limit of his campaign, perhaps on the site of an Achaeminid settlement named for Cyrus. After Alexander's death in 323 BCE, his successor in Syria and Persia, Seleucus I, established and maintained a Greek population in the region, although in the late fourth century BCE (*ca.* 305–303), he signed a treaty with King Chandragupta Maurya (in classical sources, Sandrokottos) after which Arachosia and other settlements became part of the Indian Maurya Empire.[93] These regions were settled by a variety of ethnicities and cultures, and the surviving material culture reveals a range of glocalizing practices. Inscriptions in multiple languages (Prakrit, Greek, and Aramaic) describe the Mauryan king Asoka's promotion of Buddhism and his diplomatic missions as far as Albania and Sri Lanka; bilingual coins in Greek and Indian scripts, intended for use in trading with the populations of the Hindu Kush and Gandhara, present images of Vaishnava gods. Members of local elites dedicated epigrams in elegiac couplets using an erudite, archaizing Greek.[94]

A great deal of evidence for local cultural expressions has come from the site of Ai Khanoum, the most thoroughly excavated Bactrian city to date. This settlement, whose ancient name is lost, is in northern Afghanistan at the confluence of the Kokcha and the Amu Dar'ya Rivers, near the border with Tajikistan. The date of its foundation is disputed, with some scholars claiming the late fourth century BCE, and others claiming that the older parts of the site were built during the reign of the Seleucid king Antiochus I Soter (281–261 BCE).[95] For over a century, the city was one of the principal settlements of Greco-Bactria, before being abandoned in the middle of the second century (*ca.* 145 BCE). The excavation of Ai Khanoum between 1964 and 1978 by the team from the French Archaeological Delegation in Afghanistan

(DAFA) led by Paul Bernard uncovered evidence for a wide economic and cultural network that included the Hellenic Mediterranean, the Indian subcontinent, and the Eurasian steppes.[96] The site offers an opportunity to study the constructed relationships between the Greco-Bactrian world and its individual settlements. While the rulers of Bactria were careful to project an overwhelmingly Hellenic self-image in their inscriptions and public works, it is possible to observe a complex intermingling of local traditions among the names, writings, and religious practices of the inhabitants at Ai Khanoum. Rachel Mairs has explained this range of cultural influences as a selective and ordered process of identity production by local elites attempting to define and claim Greek identity. Drawing from Barth's definition of ethnicity, Mairs has argued that the construction of Greco-Bactrian identity was "a dynamic process, asserted through public display architecture, ritual and inscriptions."[97]

In certain contexts, the architecture of Ai Khanoum has many features typical of a Hellenic city.[98] In addition to an agora and an acropolis, the city has a theater on the scale of the one at Epidauros, capable of accommodating an audience of 5,000–6,000.[99] Built into the slope of the acropolis, the theater resembles Greek examples, except for the building materials and the presence of three loggias, which Rapin reads as evidence for a highly stratified society. The city's theatrical culture is illustrated by an architectural decoration taken from a fountain house in the image of a dramatic mask, which Bernard and Rapin associate with Athenian New Comedy, and by the discovery of a literary text in dramatic verse that mentions Dionysus, which Douglas Olson has argued belongs to an unknown play by Sophocles.[100] On the bank of the Amu Dar'ya on the northern extremity of the urban center is another characteristically Hellenic building, identified by a majority of scholars as a gymnasium on account of a limestone dedicatory inscription to Hermes and Heracles commissioned by two brothers, Triballos (an ethnic name from northern Thrace) and Straton (attested in other texts at the site as well as among Greco-Bactrian sovereigns).[101] Both names suggest that the brothers are descendants of Alexander's soldiers. Given the shape and size of the building, approximately 100 m² with a series of rooms and columned exedras surrounding a central courtyard, the building resembles well-known palaestrae at Olympia and Delphi and conforms to Vitruvius' description of a palaestra in his treatise *On Architecture* (5.11). As at Olympia, Ai Khanoum's gymnasium-palaestra complex appears to have been built along the riverbank that forms the western boundary of the site. If correctly identified, the palaestra would have provided a setting for education and social interaction as well as athletic training and competition in a style characteristic of the Hellenic polis.[102]

The city's shrine (*heroon*) to its founder, Kineas, located in the necropolis outside the city walls, is a third site of constructed Hellenic identity. In the *pronaos* of the colonnaded shrine, Bernard's team discovered part of an inscription of Delphic maxims, with an accompanying epigram in a highly allusive literary style:[103]

> These wise [sayings] of the ancients, words of the far-famed, are dedicated in holy Delphi. Recording these thoughtfully from that place, Clearchus dedicated them, far-shining, in the sanctuary of Kineas: "as a boy, be well-behaved [κόσμιος], as a youth be self-controlled [ἐγκρατής], in middle-age be just [δίκαιος], as an elder be good in council [εὔβουλος], [and] at one's death be free from sorrow or regret.

The stele preserves six (143–147) of the 150 maxims known to us from Stobaeus's list, with two textual differences: the manuscripts of Stobaeus preserve ἴσθι instead of Clearchus's γίνου and advised elders to be "well-spoken" (εὔλογος) instead of "good in council" (εὔβουλος).[104] Some have identified the Clearchus of the Delphic inscription with Clearchus of Soli, an Aristotelian philosopher who is believed to have traveled through India in the late fourth century BCE. However, this almost universally accepted identification rests on very little evidence, and Lerner and Mairs have argued on chronological and archaeological grounds that it is most likely false.[105] Even in its fragmentary condition, the brief text is a fascinating cultural *mélange*. It presumes knowledge of and interest in Hellenic literary, philosophical, and religious culture. As Adrian Hollis has shown, the prefatory epigram contains echoes of Homer, Pindar, Parmenides, and Apollonius of Rhodes, as well as a fascination with rare forms characteristic of the learned Hellenistic (Alexandrian) poets.[106] The public display of these maxims in a local context of symbolic significance also reveals the desire of the Macedonian colonists and their descendants at Ai Khanoum to make claims to their Hellenic identity. Mairs associates the dedication with a mid-second-century urban renovation undertaken by "the Bactrian-born generation," for whom Clearchus' journey to Delphi was part of a symbolic refoundation that emphasized the city's Hellenic identity.[107]

The inscription is also in dialogue with the local religious traditions of India, especially the Mauryan king Asoka's bilingual "Rock Edicts," which translate Buddhist religious precepts into Greek. The texts share an interest, for example, in "self-control" (ἐγκράτια). In the twelfth edict, Asoka's text translates *guti-* in the compound *vacaguti-* ("restrained in speech") with the Greek ἐγκρατής. David Sick explains this parallel in terms of the long history of asceticism in Indian culture. Asoka's edicts make self-control a central concern of religious and philosophical education, expanding the concept of *dhamma* beyond Greek "piety" (εὐσεβία) to include aspects of "moderation" (σωφροσύνη).[108] Claiming that the Delphic inscription predated the Rock Edicts, Yailenko concluded that Asoka's concept of *dhamma* had been influenced by Greek ethical philosophies, but the relative chronology cannot be proven.[109] On the contrary, one feature of Clearchus' inscription suggests the opposite. Asoka's twelfth edict remarks that "whosoever is in control of his tongue is most in control of himself" (ἐγκρατὴς δὲ μάλιστά ἐστιν ὃς ἂν γλώσ(σ)ης ἐγκρατὴς ᾖ). Sick cites parallel thoughts in Buddhist scriptures and proverbs that recommend self-control in speaking, including some attributed to Gautama Buddha himself, and he compares them with Pythagorean practices, which included extended periods of ritual silence.[110] Especially striking in this regard is a passage from the reconstructed work, *On the Races of India and the Brahmans* (*De gentibus Indiae et Bragmanibus*), preserved among the writings of the fifth century CE bishop Palladius of Helenopolis. In the passage, which Sick reads as an indictment of the Greek philosophical tradition writ large, a group of Brahmans in dialogue with Alexander the Great complain that the Greeks simply talk too much: "for your mind is your tongue and your thoughts are always upon your lips" (2.8).[111] Could this Buddhist critique of Greek culture explain Clearchus' substitution in the Delphic maxims of εὔβουλος for εὔλογος, which Stobaeus' text preserves as the virtue of an older man? Perhaps the inscription's author, being aware of the Buddhist virtue of restrained speech (*vacaguti-*), chose to replace a Greek word associated with speech with one that might appeal to local sensibilities. If the suggestion strikes readers as plausible, it would suggest that Clearchus' inscription reflected Buddhist principles (as inscribed by Asoka) and not the other way around.

Not all public areas of Ai Khanoum make such overt claims to Hellenic identity. The administrative and religious culture of the city reveals the blending of local traditions and practices that one might expect from a multicultural settlement. The palace, or administrative center, was built in the style of Achaemenid palaces at Susa and Persepolis (themselves modeled on Mesopotamian palaces, such as Babylon's). Alongside the flat roof and brick construction, the city's Greco-Bactrian architects included Hellenic features, such as a bath and a portico. Rapin concluded that the Macedonian settlers imposed military and political control without overriding or destroying the local traditions, a sentiment that reflects the spirit of glocalization.[112] Records of accounts and transactions inscribed on *ostraka* and preserved in Ai Khanoum's treasury contain Greek names, including Zenon, Timodemus, Straton, and Philiskos, Greek settlers from Macedonia, Thessaly, and Thrace, alongside the names of local Bactrians, like Ātur, Oxèboakès, Aryandès, and Xatrannos, creating the appearance of a mixed central administration.[113]

A final example of the cultural *mélange* at Ai Khanoum is the main religious building, which adopts a Mesopotamian architectural plan alongside features that indicate a fusion of Greco-Bactrian religious practice. The building has come to be known as the "Temple with Indented Niches," referring to the indentations along its exterior walls.[114] Mairs has argued that the temple's Mesopotamian form has its origin in Achaemenid Bactria and can be studied alongside the city's other institutions to show how the residents used different locations to express ethic and cultural identities. The surviving materials within the temple reveal a variety of cultural and religious practices, suggesting a blending of cultures. The fragments from the left foot of a cult statue (only parts of the hands and feet survive), for instance, show a sandal with winged thunderbolts, which led Bernard and others to identify it as an incarnation of Zeus, possibly syncretized with a local sky god.[115] The thirty upturned vases buried in an old stratum at the rear of the temple contain traces of liquid offerings, which are consistent with chthonic cult activity in the Hellenic world as well as in Central Asia.[116] Other artifacts seem more rooted in distinct identities. A limestone sculpture of an athletic youth wearing a crown of leaves with two ribbons descending his upper back was found in the temple, in which Bernard perceived the influence of Lysippus.[117] Few objects evoke upper-class Hellenic identity more than nude athletic sculptures bearing garlands. Mairs' survey of the temple and its surroundings supports the thesis that "Greekness" at Ai Khanoum was a constructed identity, strongly asserted in certain contexts.

The intertwining at Ai Khanoum of Panhellenic and Indo-Bactrian cultural expressions is striking, revealing a variety of glocalizing practices.[118] Some facilities and institutions (like the palaestra and the theater) claim Hellenic identity in their design, while others demonstrate a synthesis of transregional styles (like the administrative palace and the temple). A few, including the inscription of the Delphic maxims, may even permit multiple simultaneous readings by audiences from different cultural traditions. The reorientation of local in relation to global reveals how the influences and effects of globalization are multidirectional, with local expressions of culture responding to and in turn helping to shape regional and transregional identities. Glocalizing approaches address Eurocentrism in ancient history by destabilizing the conceptual "centers" of the field and encouraging scholars to rethink the relationship between local and transregional processes. Hellenistic Bactria is a splendid example because of its diversity of multidirectional cultural forces. In one context, an Indian man, Subhuti son of Narada, claims for himself a Greek name (Sophytos son of Naratos) and commissions a highly allusive literary epigram in Greek, presenting himself and his family as thoroughly Hellenic. In another, a Greek man, Heliodorus son of Dion, dedicates an Indian-style pillar with an inscription in Prakrit, claiming for himself an Indian name (Heliodora son of Diya) and presenting himself in terms of Indian religion and ritual.[119] As Mairs cautions, however, though the city has received a great deal of attention due to its long and spectacular history of excavation, it should not be treated as representative of the region.[120] We also should not imagine Ai Khanoum as a transcultural utopia. While the site reveals much about constructions of greekness in Hellenistic Bactria, it cannot tell us about the receptions of greekness by the native populations. How did native Bactrians respond to the inscription of the Delphic maxims? What did they think of the gymnasium-palaestra and what went on there? How did they feel about Clearchus' mission to Delphi as part of a ritual refoundation of the colony? Behind these questions lie all too familiar anxieties about how occidentalist-Eurocentric traditions of archaeology and art history condition scholars to privilege Hellenic cultural expressions at the expense of others.

All too often, glocalizing practices are considered instances of hellenization. One popular history imagined the local population competing to join the Hellenic gymnasium, "like Indians under the British Raj angling for the *entrée* to European club membership."[121] The occidentalism in this remark draws from ancient sentiments such as those by Plutarch, whose treatise *On the Great Fortune or the Virtue of Alexander* extolls Alexander's civilizing mission in Asia. In Plutarch's account, by sharing Hellenic literature (328d), establishing Hellenic religion, and founding cities with Hellenic magistracies (328e), Alexander extinguished "the savagery" (329a1) in Bactria and Sogdiana. Those he conquered were "more blessed" (328e7) than those who escaped, since Alexander "compelled them to prosper, while the others had no one to put an end to their wretched lives" (328e8–328e9). Plutarch credits Alexander with fostering a sense of cosmopolitanism by sharing the gifts of Hellenic culture: "he commanded them all to consider the whole inhabited earth [τὴν οἰκουμένην] as their fatherland" (329c5).

The same mentality has informed historical narratives that place the end of Hellenic Bactria in the middle of the second century BCE. Writing not long after the invasion by the Yueh-chi in 135–130 BCE, Polybius imagined the *rapprochement* in 206 BCE between the Seleucid king Antiochus III and the secessionist ruler of Bactria, Euthydemus. In the fictitious dialogue, Euthydemus argues that neither kingdom will be safe unless Antiochus accepts Bactrian independence: "for not a few multitudes of Nomads are at hand, who pose a threat to both, and the land will assuredly be barbarized [ἐκβαρβαρωθήσεσθαι] if they are permitted to enter" (11.34.5). Santo Mazzarino saw in this passage Polybius' horrified response to what he felt was the destruction of Hellenic Bactria, framed as Euthydemus' prophetic words to Antiochus. In Mazzarino's reading, the "flood" and "wave" of invaders, which "submerged" eastern Iran, anticipated by six centuries the later migration of Goths into the Roman Empire.[122] Bactria's barbarization, as imagined by Polybius and generalized into a principal of global history by

Transborder 41

Mazzarino, is the conceptual inverse of the Eurocentric concept of Bactria's hellenization as imagined by Plutarch. As we have seen, however, the Hellenic culture of Greco-Bactria was carefully and unevenly constructed as one of a series of transcultural syncretisms that included reciprocal influences of hellenization, indianization, sanskritization, and iranization.[123] The image of the invading barbarian hordes bringing destruction to the civilized world requires as much adjustment as the images of cultural homogenization and the destruction of differences through globalization. In like manner, the related idea of the end of the ancient world, which forms the central theme of Mazzarino's book, requires revision. We will undertake that task in the next chapter.

Conclusion

This chapter has made a case for a decentered, deterritorialized approach to antiquity by showing how territorial boundaries are fluid and vulnerable to globalizing processes. These processes, commonly involving the movements of goods, people, and ideas across bordered space, are characteristic of the discourse of the global. They can be recognized and studied through research that considers the relationship between the local, regional, and superregional. In bringing global theory into classical studies, scholars have focused on its decentering mode, especially as it plays out in the dynamics of center-periphery and local-global.

As a natural consequence of its panancient orientation, global classics involves thinking beyond the disciplinary construction, "Greece and Rome". In popular histories of antiquity, this phrase functions as shorthand for the ancient cultural zone defined regionally by the Italic and southern Balkan peninsulas and the surrounding islands and coastlines.[124] While the phrase remains a popular means of encoding certain kinds of knowledge about the past, it also misleads in several ways: by borrowing from modernity a reductive and anachronistic impression of fixed nations and bounded societies, by directing focus to cultural centers that do not reflect the diversity and multicentrism of ancient lifeways, and by excluding the vast expanses of the ancient world that were interconnected with the Hellenic cities and later with the Romans. Greece and Rome is vitiated by the 30,000-mile perspective, which focuses on the cultural capitals that are at the center of elite life and sustains the homogenization thesis of globalization.[125] This view from above, which universalizes the perspective and experience of the contemporary world's transnational elite, is characteristic of studies of imperialism: exaggerating the influence of metropolises and urban centers and devaluing the roles of localities in processes of social change. The tendency to essentialize and generalize peoples in antiquity, by reducing them to conceptual groupings with a city at their center, is a significant obstacle to the globalization of classics, ancient history, and archaeology.

Global theory permits a wider and more inclusive approach, supplementing the study of Greece and Rome with multicentric, comparative approaches to ancient worlds. Robert Witcher has addressed the privileged status of the Roman Empire in contemporary globalizing ideologies in order to "provincialize" Roman globalization in ways that may facilitate comparison with other ancient globalizations, especially in India and China.[126] In his decentering account, Roman globalization emerges as a glocalized form of Hellenic culture, itself a marginalized and impoverished region on the margins of an older, wealthier, and more powerful eastern Mediterranean network. Scholars working in several subdisciplines have pushed these boundaries by suggesting new transborder methods for understanding antiquity, including comparative historical studies of slavery, colonization, and empire.[127] Witcher's attempt to provincialize Roman globalization reflects the work of postcolonial and subaltern studies to write alternative cultural histories against Eurocentrism.[128]

The challenge of synthesizing diverse cultural and literary histories is answered in part by the development of the field of world literature, which studies modes of circulation and of reading applied to individual works or to large groups of works.[129] This characterization reflects the contrast with which this chapter opened between internationalism and globalism.[130] Pascale Casanova's world republic of letters reflects the international approach, in which national literary traditions are still relevant for theorizing literary production and no country's literature is free from the influence of international commerce and competition.[131] Casanova critiques postcolonialism for ignoring literature's true worldliness (the "aesthetic, formal or stylistic characteristics that actually 'make' literature") in favor of its political and historical specificity.[132] Pheng Cheah responds by observing that Casanova's transnational literary world reproduces the governing forces of international politics, with its laws, revolutions, markets, and economies.[133] In contrast, globalism imagines forms of cultural production and exchange that transcend, avoid, ignore, or dismiss nations. Gayatri Spivak's concept of planetarity and Paul Gilroy's study of black counterculture are examples of transnational and antinational literary discourses.[134]

Mobilizing these paradigms in the study of ancient texts, Alexander Beecroft has introduced the concept of literary ecologies to describe the conditions that govern the growth and circulation of local (epichoric) texts and ideas into national (panchoric) and transnational (cosmopolitan and global) literatures.[135] Beecroft explains the panhellenization of ancient texts in terms that are not only transborder but diachronic, something that we will discuss in the next chapter.[136] Beecroft imagines the possibility of future global ecologies of literature in terms that echo Barber's dichotomy in "Jihad vs. McWorld:" a homogenized globality of literature in a single vernacular (e.g., English) or genre (e.g., the novel) contrasted with a heterotopia of transnational literary languages, driven by technological or political developments that lower the bar of entry for individual authors and diverse languages into the world literary system.[137] In like manner, this chapter has been the story of two ways of locating the global in antiquity. One model understands globalization as large-scale, top-down, and homogenizing, effacing difference through violence or acculturation, and in this way interlinking the global history of events in a single direction. The alternative model imagines a globalization from the bottom up, emphasizing the heterogenous relations of local, regional, and transborder entities. Both narratives are part of the discourse of globalization studies, which as we have seen is best characterized in terms of a spectrum of local-global.

These interventions in the history of world literatures illustrate the temporal as well as the spatial dimensions of globalization. Wendy Doniger's comparative study of Greco-Hindu mythography, for instance, documents and compares stories of doubling and splitting in the mythological canons of ancient Greece and India using an appropriately double methodology:

> Certain features shared by the two sets of stories—such as the recurrence of equine twins in the mythologies of Saranyu, Sita, and Helen—are shared cultural assumptions that result from historical connections between Greece and India . . . On the other hand, other shared features . . . are the result of more widely shared human bonds that transcend these cultural barriers.[138]

This contrast contains an implicit, global theory of literature. The common interest in doubles across Greek and Hindu mythography may be understood by a hybrid methodology: *morphologically* in terms of the stories' formal, aesthetic, and stylistic elements (Casanova's "characteristics that actually 'make' literature," discussed previously) and *historically* in the context of stories of contact and exchange between Hellenic and Indian cultures. This hybrid, globalized theory of literature eschews the historicist relation of source and recipient and imagines that literature is everywhere a recipient, always already hybridized. Doniger draws from Sheldon Pollock's critique of indigenism, which "inhibits us from seeing that all literary cultures participate in what turn out to be networks, ultimately globalized networks, of borrowing, appropriating, reacting, imitating, emulating, rivaling, defeating."[139] Put in the terms of globalization, world literatures are always *glocalized* products manifesting global cultural networks in local contexts and moments. Pollock describes the notion of civilization as "an arbitrary moment . . . illegitimately generalized." The coproduction of local and global literary cultures operates on a spectrum from local and regional formations, to cosmopolitan ecumenes, and finally to transcontinental or even world systems of literary culture.[140] These multidimensional (literary) historical narratives contribute to the formation of glocal identities in ways that are crucial to the establishment of social order and, as Pollock observes, to the acquisition and maintenance of social and political power.

The model that Pollock proposes as an alternative to models of cultural diffusion, acculturation, and homogenization draws explicitly from globalization research and aims to reassert the role of the local aspect ("the radical dynamism and particularities") of premodern, global cultural flows. From this perspective, a form of the westernization model is a "permanent and global phenomenon," to the extent that "different areas have functioned as 'Wests' for different 'Easts' at different periods of history."[141] Whereas Pollock sees these relations primarily in terms of static geographies and cultural politics—"England could be said to be France's West in the sixteenth century" and "Iran functioned as India's West at various periods (Achaemenid, Sasanian)"—they also (perhaps primarily) operate across periods. Globalizing culture zones perceived (or self-declared) as older and politically, economically, or culturally superior provoke responses and consequences as emerging cultural localities draw connections and make distinctions with what they see as established traditions.[142] How can we understand the spectrum of local-global as reflecting not only multilevel spatial relations but relations in time as well? What is the relation between the arbitrary moments in the history of events and the construction of large-scale cultural histories? And what alternative cultural histories emerge from taking a transhistorical approach to the remote past? This temporal dimension of globalization is the subject of the next chapter.

Notes

1 Mittelman 2005; Nederveen Pieterse 2013.
2 Nederveen Pieterse 1995: 45; Hopkins 2002, 2010; Mittelman 2005.
3 The distinction between objective and subjective appears in Steger and Wahlrab 2017: 53.
4 Rouse 1991, 1995; Basch, Glick Schiller, and Szanton-Blanc 1994: 48; Owen 2015: 39–41.
5 Vertovec 1999, 2001; Sadowski-Smith ed. 2002; Gowricharn 2009; Khagram and Levitt eds. 2008; Nederveen Pieterse 2013: 506–507; Owen 2015.
6 Müller 2016.
7 Kearney 1995: 548.
8 Harvey 1989: 293; Cairncross 1997.
9 Castells 1996.
10 Steger 2008; Steger and Wahlrab 2017: 3–7.

11 Wallerstein 1974a, 1974b, 1980; Giddens 1990: 52 and *passim*; Robertson 1992: 58–60; Eriksen 2007: 13; Schäfer 2007; the descriptive phrase "Great Wall" appears in Jennings 2011: 4–13. Frank and Gills (1993: 9) call the break at 1500 CE world history's "Gordion knot."
12 Flynn and Giráldez 2006: 211.
13 Waters 1995: 7.
14 Wallerstein 1974a, 1974b, 1980; Robertson 1992: 58–60; Giddens 1990.
15 Wallerstein 1974a, 1974b, 1980; Chase-Dunn and Hall 1997.
16 Wallerstein 1974b: 15; Waters 1995: 37.
17 Wallerstein 1974a: 348.
18 Giddens 1990: 63 and 70–8; and discussions in Robertson 1992: 12–15; Nederveen Pieterse 1995: 46–49; Waters 1995: 61–64, 109–110.
19 Hopkins 1999.
20 Hopkins 2002.
21 Discussion in Pitts and Versluys 2015a: 15–16; Nederveen Pieterse 2015: 226–227.
22 Nederveen Pieterse 1995; Gilroy 1993.
23 Gilroy 1993; Nederveen Pieterse 1995: 47; cf. Bentley 2004: 77.
24 Abu-Lughod 1989, 1993.
25 The term "globalization" does not appear in Abu-Lughod 1989, which uses the phrase "world system" (unhyphenated) instead. See also Frank and Gills 1993; Ekholm and Friedman 1993; Wilkinson 1993; Nederveen Pieterse 2015: 226.
26 Chakrabarty (2000).
27 Diop 1955, 1967, 1981; Obenga 1995; ben-Jochannan 1988; Dominick 2007.
28 Bernal 1987; Amin 1989, 1993; and discussion in Frank and Gills 1993: 11–12.
29 Frank and Gills 1993: 11.
30 Wilkinson 1993: 226.
31 Duncan 2011; Bosher 2012; Stewart 2017. The quotes are from Carter 2007: 19, but similar views are expressed by, for example, Rehm 1989: 32–33; Goldhill 1987, 2000; Burian 2011; P. Wilson 2011. For objections along different grounds, see Connor 1989; Rhodes 2003.
32 Wilson 1993; Newlands 2002; Pomeroy 2003; Henderson 2007; Pogorzelski 2016.
33 E. Hall 1989; cf. Kuhrt and Sherwin-White eds. 1987; Miller 1997.
34 Parker 2002; Loar, MacDonald, and Padilla Peralta 2018.
35 Vasunia 2001.
36 Moyer 2011; Haubold 2013.
37 Dougherty and Kurke 2003.
38 Wijma 2014; Kennedy 2014; Vasunia 2001; Haubold 2013; Kasimis 2018, 2020.
39 Bagnall 1995; Bagnall and Cribiore 2006.
40 Barth 1969.
41 van Dommelen and Knapp 2010: 4.
42 Hopkins 1978; Rowlands 1987; Cunliffe 1988; and discussion in Pitts and Versluys 2015a: 9–10.
43 Woolf 1997, 1998; discussions in Jiménez 2010, Pitts and Versluys 2015a: 5–6.
44 Shaw 2001: 453.
45 For example, Morris 2003; Harris ed. 2005; Malkin ed. 2005, 2011; Hodos 2006; Vlassopoulos 2007.

46 *Transborder*

46 Morris 2003. Cf. Harris ed. 2005; Malkin ed. 2005.
47 Malkin 2011.
48 Malkin 2011: 40–1, 207; Gras 1995.
49 Vlassopoulos 2007: 8.
50 Vlassopoulos 2007, 2013; Taylor and Vlassopoulos 2015.
51 Vlassopoulos 2013: 19–20.
52 Robertson 1992; Appadurai 2000; Vlassopoulos 2013: 19–32 and ch.6; see discussion to follow.
53 Vlassopoulos 2013: 21; Müller 2016: 3.
54 Malitz 2000; Witcher 2000, 2017; Fusco 2003; Alonso-Núñez 2004; Sfameni Gasparro 2004–5; Pitts and Versluys eds. 2015b.
55 See Pitts and Versluys 2015b: 5–6, and discussions of romanization in Millett 1990; Woolf 1998.
56 Hingley 2005, 2011, 2015.
57 Naerebout 2006–2007.
58 Hitchner 2008: 2–3.
59 Hitchner 2008: 2; Hingley 2015: 42.
60 Pitts and Versluys eds. 2015b; Hodos ed. 2017a. For religion, see Woolf 2005; Petzold, Rüpke, and Steimle 2001. For mobility and connectivity, see Laurence and Trifilò 2015; Isayev 2015; Hodos 2015. For the ancient economy, see Vlassopoulos 2007: ch.5; Morley 2015; Pitts 2015. For material culture and identity, see Parker 2002; Sweetman 2007; Hodos 2006, 2010a; van Dommelen and Knapp 2010; Jiménez 2010; Versluys 2015.
61 Mayhew 1995; Vlassopoulos 2007: ch.8.
62 McCarthy 2003; Inglis and Robertson 2004: 170–172.
63 Inglis and Robertson 2004, 2005.
64 Polybius calls Ephorus the "first and only who has undertaken to write the affairs of the whole world [τὰ καθόλου]" (5.33.2). Diodorus Siculus (16.76 = Ephorus *BNJ* 70 T10) notes that the final event in his narrative was the siege of Perinthus in 340–339 BCE (cf. Philochorus, *BNJ* 368 T54). See Marincola 2008: 399–404; Parmeggiani 2011.
65 Alonso-Núñez 1990: 177; Clarke 1999: 100 n.52. Isocrates' name appears in Strabo (13.3.6), Cicero (*De Oratore* 2.94), Seneca (*De tranquilitate animi* 7.2), and Diodorus Siculus (4.1.2).
66 See Diodorus Siculus 5.1.4. On κατὰ γένος, see Drews 1963; Parmeggiani 2011: 156–159 with bibliography. Marincola (2008: 400) contrasts Thucydides "annalistic" arrangement.
67 Strabo (10.3.5); cf. Polybius (34.1.3).
68 Drews 1963; Clarke 1999: 121–122 and 156–157.
69 5.20.5, with criticisms at, for example, 6.45.1. See Walbank 1957: *ad loc*. On Polybius' defense of Ephorus against Timaeus, see Baron 2013: 61–63.
70 Cf. 1.4.7.
71 Alonso-Núñez 2004: 9.
72 Inglis and Robertson 2005.
73 Inglis and Robertson 2004: 179.
74 Polybius explains in the prologue to Book 3 (3.4) his decision to extend the work by 22 years, covering in the final ten books (30–39) the rebellion and destruction of the Achaean league, which culminated in 146 BCE.
75 Vlassopoulos 2007: 122.
76 Walbank 1967: *ad loc*.

77 Walbank 2002: 184–190.
78 Drews 1963; Alonso-Núñez 1990.
79 Benjamin 2014: 360.
80 Clarke 1999: 101.
81 Sommer 2015: 182.
82 *Ibid.* 187–191.
83 For the date, see Fontanella 2007: 79.
84 Robertson 1995; Appadurai 2000; Vlassopoulos 2013: ch.6; Steger and Wahlrab 2017: 60.
85 Appadurai 1990: 295.
86 Ferguson 1992: 80.
87 E.g. Morris 2003; Malkin 2011.
88 Barber 1992.
89 Robertson 1995: 34.
90 Cf. McNeil 1985.
91 Vlassopoulos 2013: ch.6.
92 For the region, its history, and its archaeology, readers should consult Tarn 1938; Holt 1999, 2012; Mairs 2011.
93 Just. *Epit.* 15.4.20. Tarn 1938: 100; Holt 1999: 28; Kosmin 2014: 32–37.
94 Di Castro 2005: 6; Austin 2006: 313; Mairs 2008: 29–37; Hollis 2011: 112–116; Wallace 2016: 219–222.
95 Mairs 2013, 2014: ch.2; Martinez-Sève 2014: 270 and 2015; Wallace 2016.
96 Rapin 1996; Lerner 2003; Mairs 2008: 28.
97 Mairs 2008: 22; cf. Barth 1969.
98 Holt (1999: 44) lists finds including "a Macedonian palace, Rhodian porticoes, Coan funerary monuments, an Athenian propylaea, Delian houses, Megarian bowls, Corinthian tiles, and Mediterranean amphorae."
99 Bernard 1980: 429–441; Rapin 1990: 338.
100 Bernard 1976: 311–313; Rapin 1990: 339. For the dramatic fragment, see Hollis 2011: 107–109; Olson 2019.
101 Canali De Rossi 2004: 223, #381.
102 Bernard 1976: 293–302, 1978: 421–429.
103 Canali De Rossi 2004: 224–227, #382 and 384. See Moore 2020: 291–297.
104 For Stobaeus' text, see Wachsmuth and Hense 1884–1894: 3.173 (pp. 125–128).
105 In favor of this attribution, Rapin 1990: 339; Holt 1999: 158; Austin 2006: 314–315; Kosmin 2014: 64 and 237–238; critiques of these views in Lerner 2003–2004: 393–394; Mairs 2015; Martinez-Sève 2015: 32 n.80; Wallace 2016: 217. For Clearchus of Soli's interests in Indian philosophy, see Diogenes Laertius 1.9.
106 Hollis 2011: 109–110, who also discusses (114) the intertextualities of Sophytos' funerary epigram from Kandahar with Callimachus' *Hecale*; Wallace 2016: 216 (and 219–221 for Sophytos' inscription).
107 Mairs 2013: 105–106, 2015: 122; Wallace 2016: 217–219.
108 Sick 2007: 261–262.
109 Yailenko 1990: 250; Sick 2007: 263.
110 Sick 2007: 263–268.
111 Sick 2007: 265–266. For Palladius' text, see Berghoff 1967. As if in acknowledgment of this feature of Greek philosophical literature, a parchment found at Ai Khanoum preserves part of a disputatious philosophical dialogue in Platonic style, with a speaker and an interlocutor who responds in brief affirmations or denials. Bernard 1980: 456–458 and fig. 20; Rapin 1990: 339 and plate 37.3; Lerner 2003.

48 *Transborder*

112 Rapin 1990: 338; cf. Di Castro 2005: 5.
113 Rapin and Grenet 1983: #3, 4a-b, 4c, 7, 15; Wallace 2016: 224.
114 For the temple, see Bernard 1969: 327–355; Mairs 2008: 28–29, 2013.
115 Bernard 1969: 340.
116 Mairs 2013: 94–95. For the discovery of the vases, see Bernard 1970: 327–330.
117 Bernard 1969: 341–344.
118 Vlassopoulos 2013: 296.
119 Mairs 2008: 35; Hollis 2011: 112–116; Wallace 2016: 219–223.
120 Mairs 2008: 27.
121 Green 1990: 116.
122 Mazzarino 1966: 25–26; critiques of this view in Walbank 1957–1979: *ad* 9.34.5; Di Castro 2005: 2–3.
123 Di Castro 2005: 11–12.
124 For example, Spawforth 2018.
125 Nederveen Pieterse 2013: 510.
126 Witcher 2017; cf. Doniger 1999; Beecroft 2010; Denecke 2014.
127 Mutschler and Mittag 2008; Fynn-Paul 2009; Scheidel ed. 2009; Hodos 2010b; van Dommelen 2012.
128 For example, Chakrabarty 2000; see discussion at the conclusion of Chapter 2.
129 Damrosch 2003: 4.
130 Kalliney 2016: 162–163.
131 Casanova 2004: 164–172.
132 Casanova 2005: 71.
133 Cheah 2016: 32.
134 Spivak 2003: ch.3; Gilroy 1993: 29–40.
135 Beecroft 2015.
136 For diachronicity see González ed. 2015, and discussion in Chapter 2.
137 Beecroft 2015: 249–250, 279, 295–296.
138 Doniger 1999: 4.
139 Pollock 1995: 136.
140 *Ibid.* 112.
141 *Ibid.* 135.
142 The dynamic between an aspiring hegemonic state and an older, neighboring civilization is the subject of Denecke 2014; cf. Witcher 2017.

2 Transhistorical

The previous chapter presented evidence for a decentered approach to antiquity focusing on the dynamic between the experiences of locality and the perceptions of globality. It sought to understand classical research in terms of processes that cross territorial boundaries and, by drawing on the work of comparative cultural studies, to imagine what the study of a global antiquity might look like. But globalizing classics depends on more than deterritorializing our understanding of antiquity by emphasizing transregional processes and identities. The debate among historians of globalization about where and when globalization began, and how periods characterized as globalizing differ from those that are not, reflects the importance of rethinking how we construct and study the record of human activity and events through time. This chapter presents approaches to the hyperfragmented, periodic boundaries both within antiquity and between antiquity and today. Just as transnational thinking involves questioning territorial borders, transhistorical thinking involves challenging temporal contours, periodic boundaries, and chronologies and even questioning the notion of "antiquity" itself. It encourages us to recognize that boundaries in time are as malleable and permeable by globalizing processes as spatial, geopolitical boundaries and to rethink the relationship between periodization and sociocultural change.

The first subsection attempts to provide an account of the concept of transhistoricism that distinguishes it from diachrony and describes how it helps us to rethink periodization in and since antiquity.[1] Although the phrases "space-time compression" and "annihilation of space through time" feature among the most common definitions of globalization, it is the concept of "space" that has received the majority of theoretical attention.[2] That is, even though globalization is frequently understood as processual and unfolding over time, less critical thought has been given to the role that the perceived passage of time (perceived, that is, at various scales) plays in our constructions of the global past and present. Transhistorical questions involve the dynamics of reconstructing social transformations over time: if globalization is to be understood as a process of social change, then what constitutive units demarcate the process, and how do we interrelate them to produce historical narratives about the global past and connect it with the present? Borrowing from archaeological theory and adopting a postcolonial outlook, this section considers the fragmentation of the past into periods and ages and investigates the tension between the aspiration to represent and appreciate the diversity of historical outlooks and perspectives and the desire to integrate this diversity into larger, global narratives. Transhistorical thinking allows us to reimagine our practices of periodization and chronology, while adding a degree of flexibility and adaptability to our histories of the ancient world.

The second section examines two subfields of classical scholarship that put this modality to work. Studies in the classical tradition chronicle the dissemination of classical texts and ideas in postclassical periods, especially through education. Studies in classical receptions document how artifacts of past societies (texts, objects, ideas) are received, rewritten, reperformed, reinterpreted, copied, remade, adapted, and otherwise appropriated by their own and later cultures. Both fields aim to link ideas and artifacts across the borders that separate the perceived, unified periods of human historical time. Both have also made claims to the term global, in that they address engagement around the world with the ideas and artifacts of ancient Greco-Roman cultures. These methodologies reflect the spectrum of local-global that is a defining feature of global studies. Transhistorical thinking allows us to globalize the field by acknowledging the variety of ways that the past survives in an enduring present.

Time and place

One pithy definition of globalization claims that it refers to "the expansion and intensification of social relations and consciousness across world-time and world-space."[3] The six elements featured in this formulation require unpacking. They can be understood as capturing two contrasting orientations toward globalization, reflected in the following lists of terms:

expansion	intensification
social relations	(social) consciousness
world-space	world-time
observed	perceived
objective	subjective

The first pair, expansion and intensification, denote contrasting processes of growth over time. But whereas expansion is a term of physical volume that can be observed, measured, and calculated, intensification must be felt, perceived, and described. The contrast is more fully developed in the second pairing: social relations, which reflects the chief interest of the social sciences in transactional dynamics of globalization, and consciousness, which draws meaning from human creative expression, thought, and language. One way to characterize the difference between studies of globalization and global studies is to observe that the former (including in ancient history and archaeology) is oriented toward the first column, whereas the latter emerges from a dialectic involving both columns. Programmatic descriptions of global studies make an effort to include both.[4] We will explore the importance of multidimensional, transdisciplinary approaches in the next chapter. For the moment, it will advance our discussion to observe that world-space seems to accord with the contents of the first column, leaving us to try to understand how and why world-time should accord with the second. The view that I will present in this chapter is that globalization is transhistorical and that world-time describes its processual nature.

In his *Studies in Historiography*, Momigliano reflected on the diversity of temporalities involved in writing ancient history:

> When I want to understand Italian history I catch a train and go to Ravenna. There, between the tomb of Theodoric and that of Dante, in the reassuring neighborhood of the best manuscript of Aristophanes and in the less reassuring one of the best portrait of the Empress Theodora, I can begin to feel what Italian history has really been.[5]

These artifacts encapsulated determining features of Italian history, "the presence of a foreign rule, the memory of an imperial and pagan past, and the overwhelming force of the Catholic tradition." History is what the author "begin[s] to feel," emerging from the artifacts, from their relative positions in space and time and from the scholar's journey to be in their presence. Momigliano's story of Italy springs from the perception of particularity and from movement through space. In an important section of *The Corrupting Sea*, Horden and Purcell use Momigliano's description of Ravenna as an example of "the exquisite particularities of culture and politics" that characterize the Mediterranean.[6] Building on Birot's characterization of the Mediterranean world as, "a mosaic in which the mean size of each homogenous unity is on the order of ten kilometers," Horden and Purcell present their case for the hyperfragmentation of the Mediterranean: "the almost absurd variability of the broken topography in which every slope or terrace of a valley-side, each hollow, dune and pool of a coastal lowland, may have its own identity."[7] These distinctive identities (which Horden and Purcell call microecologies) in turn derive from a combination of each locality's productive opportunities (for farming, herding, hunting, fishing, mining, commerce, etc.) with the particular set of human responses to these opportunities in a given period.

For Horden and Purcell, this sociospatial density is one of the Mediterranean's unique features, but that is not the point of interest here. Rather, Momigliano's reflection on the nature of Italian history is a construction in *time* as well as *place*, two concepts that have long been conceptualized in terms of one another. Indeed, they are rarely separated.[8] Horden and Purcell's characterization of microecologies as culturally constituted landscapes reflects decades of critical and archaeological theory defining "place" in relation to "space."[9] The literature is vast, but the spatial theories of Henri Lefebvre and Edward Soja loom large over the field. Among Lefebvre's pioneering insights was the formulation of space as a social category, not abstract and inert but a changeable medium for human relations, which both governs and responds to those relations. This reciprocal relationship between space and culture allowed him to imagine "on the horizon" large-scale social change in global terms: "the creation (or production) of a planet-wide space as the social foundation of a transformed everyday life."[10] Soja synthesizes Lefebvre's triad of perceived-conceived-lived space into three complementary epistemologies of space. The first and second reflect, respectively, the objective-analytical orientation of the social sciences and the subjective-ideational orientation of the arts. Taken together, these complementary modalities presume an epistemological completeness that "channels the accumulation of spatial knowledge into two main streams or some selective combination of both."[11] Adapting from Lefebvre and from Proust, Soja theorizes the third epistemology of space as a "remembrance-rethinking-recovery of spaces lost . . . or never sighted at all."[12]

Major thinkers in global studies have built their approaches to globalization on these spatial theories. Roland Robertson's efforts to introduce the concept of glocalization into social theory reflect both the complex interplay of global and local forces in a shrinking world and the need to bring attention to "the intimate links between temporal and spatial dimensions of human life" into the discourse of the social sciences.[13] Consequently, a majority of globalization theories are preoccupied with spatial dynamics, including empires, ecumenes, zones, world-systems, world-economies, networks, cities, and other organized spatial entities where globalizing processes (like interconnectivity and shared social consciousness) can be observed and measured.[14] A close look at the debates, described in the previous chapter, about *when* globalization began reveals that in fact they are frequently more interested *where* it began. To cite an extreme example, the argument that globalization emerged in 1571 is an argument about geography, not chronology: the key element of the argument is the foundation of Manilla, which facilitated intercontinental trade between Asia and the Americas.[15] For this reason, the presentism of globalization studies is concomitant with its Eurocentrism: the temporal and spatial focus of the field has most typically been in the particularities of time and place in post-1500 CE Europe. But even those who argue in favor of premodern globalizations build arguments about chronology on the basis of arguments about space. Abu-Lughod's arguments for a premodern world-system, for instance, are also founded more in geographies than in temporalities, built on transcontinental systems or "circuits" that connected Europe with the Middle and Far East.[16] Jennings, likewise, identifies periods of globalization in the fourth millennium BCE (and other times) by identifying the emergence of complex, sociospatial configurations like cities.[17]

Compared with the vast literature on how globalization and globality play out across space, less thought has been given to its temporal frames. This is surprising, especially in *longue durée* theories of globalization that view it in terms of flows and processes that span generations, even centuries. Almost everywhere, globality is defined in relation to both space and time. The duality is present even in the word globalization itself, in which the condition, perception, and production of increasing interconnectedness is conceived processually with the suffix "-ization," commonly used to denote a dynamic process leading to a goal.[18] One commonly cited characterization of globalization involves the shrinking or compression of the world into a single place. This idea was given shape by Hannah Arendt in *The Human Condition*, where "world alienation" is described as a "twofold flight from the earth into the universe and from the world into the self."[19] In Arendt's vision, the shared public world produced through political action is exchanged for the objectivity of scientific exploration and the subjectivity of personal introspection. Arendt associated this form of alienation with the discovery, mapping, and charting of the globe: "Speed has conquered space . . . it has made distance meaningless, for no significant part of a human life—years, months, or even weeks—is any longer necessary to reach any point on the earth."[20] Arendt's vision of apolitical cosmopolitanism draws upon the concept of the shrinking globe, linking it to the precise moment when humanity developed an "earth-wide" consciousness. The phrase "time-space compression," which is implicit also in Marshall McLuhan's description of alienation through specialization and technology, was coined by David Harvey as part of a spatial turn in globalization studies.[21] Harvey was an early critic of the popular narrative that globalization was a recent development, arguing instead that it should be understood in spatiotemporal, rather than political-economic terms. Building on core Marxian concepts, Harvey outlined the spatial relationships between use value and exchange value in order to describe how the circulation and accumulation of capital "perpetually reshapes the geographical and temporal coordinates within which we live our daily lives."[22] As a political geographer and spatial theorist influenced by Lefebvre, Harvey emphasized spatial relations, with temporalities receiving less explicit attention.

Revision of Eurocentric narratives of globalization therefore requires refocusing our temporalities as much as our geographies of the past. If the globalizing project in classics, as described in the previous chapter, can be understood as a decentering, deterritorializing, and decolonization of the discipline (understood, that is, in terms of the spaces, landscapes, and places of antiquity), then those same efforts should also be applied to its temporalities, chronologies, and intervals. Vast stretches of the human past fall within the disciplinary purview of classics and ancient history, and even greater stretches within the province of archaeology, but until recently there has been little theoretical discussion of time, as though it were an unproblematic dimension whose operations are self-evident. As a result, important questions remain about how time has been (and should be) measured and divided over the vast expanse of human events. What are its constitutive units and intervals? What is the relationship of date and chronology, and how do these concepts relate to time and to questions of social change? The acknowledgment that time is not a neutral feature in historiography invites discussion about the ethics and politics of periodization and chronology.

Classical studies has developed and grown accustomed to influential temporalities and periodizations for Greek and Roman antiquity. Though periodizations come in many forms, the most influential have been divided by significant military and political events (the Greco-Persian Wars, for instance, or the Battle of Actium) and named for significant figures or families (e.g., Age of Alexander, Neronian, Flavian) or institutional forms of government (Republican, Imperial). Drawing from admonitions by Thomas Carlyle, Thomas Mann, and Lord Acton, David Blackbourn reminds us that the formulation of periods, ages, and eras is always a human preoccupation and advises scholars of European history to be more self-conscious in their use of temporal scales.[23] In parallel, Eric Hayot offers an extensive critique from the perspective of English literary studies. Hayot's argument against institutionalized periodization demonstrates the limitations of periods as interpretive frames of reference and how these frames shape and are shaped by institutional structures and professional norms.[24] From the perspective of classics, periods are the building blocks and conceptual units of nearly all teaching and research about the ancient world, from undergraduate surveys, to graduate research, to university hiring, and beyond. My goal here is to explore the conceptual foundations and limits of established periodization schemes and to suggest some alternatives.[25]

The traditional division of ancient Greek history into Mycenaean, Dark Age, Orientalizing, archaic, classical, Hellenistic, and Roman periods is a case in point. This periodization scheme is linked to centers of cultural, political, and economic power (e.g., Mycenae and Rome) and given shape by events in military history, especially famous battles. The Persian Wars (499–479 BCE) divide the archaic and classical periods; the battle of Chaeronea (338 BCE) or the death of Alexander (323 BCE) marks the end of the classical period; and the battle of Pydna (168 BCE), the destruction of Corinth and Carthage (146 BCE), or the battle of Actium (31 BCE) divides the Hellenistic period from the Roman period. This homogenized, linear narrative is a product of the Eurocentric perspective of the past two centuries. The construction of Hellenic history as a single, national history was necessary for it to take its place as a preliminary stage in the emerging narrative of European civilization. Vlassopoulos has shown how the polis emerged as the unit that would facilitate the narrative pattern of rise, peak, and decline, while Kotsonas has revealed the political forces that have shaped the periodization of Greek archaeology.[26] Ancient history was then fashioned to resemble the familiar narrative of "Western" modernity, characterized by disruption and rediscovery. Other ancient cultures, such as the Minoan and Mycenaean, were deemed incompatible with the later development of the polis and were excluded from the chronology. Hellenic history could only begin after their destruction. Following the Dark Age in the eleventh and tenth centuries BCE, the Greeks could enjoy a renaissance of their own, a miraculous period of discovery, beginning in the ninth and eighth centuries BCE.

This chronology goes back to the eighteenth century and Winckelmann's attempt to divide Greek art history into periods, but in the centuries since then it has been largely adopted by scholars across the field. In fact, the periodization is present nowadays not only in ancient political history but in other realms of ancient activity and experience as well. This remains true despite the fact that scholars are increasingly aware that the traditional periodization does not fit either with the history of other forms of social change (economic, social, and cultural) or with archaeological evidence, which suggests that the processes of movement and habitation were uneven with significant regional variations.[27] Even in the wake of spectacular discoveries (such as those at Lefkandi in Euboea from the eleventh century BCE) that have revealed enduring cultural patterns and illuminated, for instance, the so-called Hellenic Dark Age, the phrase nevertheless persists.[28] Sarah Murray generously credits its persistence to its value as a "historical shorthand with which to quickly and forcefully communicate to students and beginners the basic (relative) cadence of early Greek history in central and southern Greece."[29] But simply adopting a new phrase to describe the period does not solve the greater problem, which remains the generally uncritical adoption of an inherited periodization scheme of limited utility.

A comparison with medieval studies is helpful here. A powerful dialectic links the idea of the Middle Ages with the ideology of modernity. The monumental study of periodization by Hans Blumenberg reinforced the rupture and discontinuity between the two periods. Because modernity "understood itself as an epoch and, in so doing, simultaneously created the other epochs," the construction of the Middle Ages played a vital role in sustaining its "legitimacy."[30] Blumenberg's thesis implies that ideologies of all kinds periodize themselves by creating discontinuity with their past, "citing, adopting, expanding, revising, and indeed even secularizing" earlier modes of thought and discourse.[31] That this process of ideology formation has an affinity with theories of reader response and reception is obvious; we will return to these theories in the next section. For now, our digression into medieval studies will be complete by observing how the ideology of modernity (the basis of many popular histories of globalization) depends on a "denial of coevalness" with the Middle Ages. The phrase, from Johannes Fabian's critique of anthropology, describes a tendency in the field to locate peoples, places, cultures, and events to another time.[32] This practice marginalizes and excludes people and groups by consigning them to other temporalities and thereby leading to injustices of other kinds.

The story of the Hellenic Dark Age (singular) parallels the Dark Ages (plural) after the fall of the western Roman Empire in the fifth and sixth centuries CE, which made way for the High Middle Ages and, eventually, for the Renaissance and modernity. The analogy was so compelling that A. R. Burn subtitled his 1936 book on Hesiod, *A Study of the Greek Middle Ages*. Its opening remarks make the analogy plain:

> Greek civilization rises on the basis of a "medieval" society of peasants and nobles, who tilled their land and very seldom traveled far afield. There was a "time of troubles" in the background; an age in which a far more brilliant society had foundered amid storms and bloodshed.[33]

The memory of earlier cultures and their decline left an impression on the poetic tradition, both in Hesiod's myth of the five ages and in Homer's narrative when Hector easily hurls a stone that two men, "such as men are today" (*Iliad* 12.449), could scarcely lift. In most ancient histories, this period of isolation and poverty comes to an end in the middle of the eighth century CE in a period that Snodgrass calls "The Greek Renaissance," characterized by new forms of interconnectivity:

> For me, the decisive moment comes when the Greek world can be seen to be moving forward *as a whole*; when the beneficial or disruptive

developments in one centre are swiftly reflected in most parts of central and southern Greece, in the islands and in Ionia. Such a state of affairs cannot be detected before the beginning of the eighth century; yet it is patently in existence before its end.[34]

Like contemporary histories of globalization, this expression of early Hellenic globality depends on a break with the past. The language resembles Flynn and Giráldez's defense of 1571 as the year when "true globalization" began: "Prior to that year, the world market was not yet fully coherent or complete; after that year it was."[35]

The problem with the Hellenic Dark Age is not with the label (though scholars are surely right to prefer early Iron Age nowadays) but rather with the practice of periodization itself. Archaeological theorists were among the first to recognize this fact, and some have challenged the practice of periodization aggressively.[36] Shanks and Tilly describe chronology as "a technology for the reduction of difference," and they offer as an example the practice of stratigraphy, which "translates variation in space into variation in time."[37] Because technologies are never neutral to power, the measurement, calculation, and division of time are political acts. Fabian's exacting critique of anthropological discourse makes this fact plain. The field's tendency to dislocate the subjects of anthropological research to a time other than that of the researcher (the "denial of coevalness" as described previously) is a colonizer's practice. Fabian demonstrates the use of contrasting temporalities to justify and legitimize colonial projects of all kinds: "temporizations expressed as passage from savagery to civilization, from peasant to industrial society, have long served an ideology whose ultimate purpose has been to justify the procurement of commodities from [African] markets."[38] The division of the ancient past into discontinuous periods and ages is an act of colonization and violence analogous to the division of the ancient world into regions, zones, and lots.[39]

In ancient Greek history, this practice displaces into other temporalities cultural histories that do not advance the linear narrative of sociopolitical progress. The treatment of Macedonian history is an obvious example of this practice. It is common to characterize Macedonian society in terms of similarities with the Homeric world that put Macedon out of step with the rest of Greece. Examples include claims by Brunt that, "Macedonian institutions too, though they resemble those we find in the Homeric poems, were alien to the Greeks of Alexander's time," or by Ellis that, "this distinctive society retained some features that seem unusual, often anachronistic, in the fourth-century context—although perhaps not so out-of-place in Homer's heroic world." Other examples include more recent statements by Holt that, "In battles, brawls, and drinking bouts, the Macedonians measured a man from king to commoner by the implacable standards of Achilles and Agamemnon," and by Gabriel that, "In many ways the Macedonia of Philip's day was very much the society of the Mycenaean age . . . where the *Iliad* was not only an ancient heroic tale but also a reflection of how men still lived."[40] These characterizations of Macedonian society as possessing alien, unusual, or anachronistic features of an earlier age illustrate the practice of denial of coevalness in ancient history and reveal the field's discomfort with the idea of a Hellenic monarchy coexisting in time with the classical form of the self-governed polis. This characterization of Macedonian society as Homeric is all the more fascinating when one factors in the wide range of opinion among scholars regarding the historicity of Homeric society. Even professional Homerists hold a wide range of opinion about when (and whether) the society depicted in the *Iliad* and *Odyssey* existed.[41] Barring some startling new discovery, the controversy is likely to continue unresolved, but my point is to show how swiftly and completely the logic of excluding the Macedonians from most of Hellenic history unravels.

The problem of periodization therefore involves a politics of representation that governs who is included in Hellenic history and who is excluded from it.[42] While narratives of cultural decline and renaissance are no longer as common as they once were, denials of coevalness endure. Among the longest suffering victims of this practice are the modern inhabitants of Greece themselves, whose rural communities were objects of condescension and embarrassment for generations.[43] Loring Danforth's critique of anthropological descriptions of rural Greece, characterized in terms of "fossilized relics of ancient Greek culture" and an "exotic anachronism," captured the field's outdated paradigms in the same terms as Fabian's interventions: "It creates a distance between them and the scholars studying them by assigning them to a different time, a time long past."[44] Confrontation of assumptions and differentiation of attitudes and approaches to the past facilitate the formation of transhistorical connections with previously marginalized cultural groups.

Recognition of the diversity of possible periodizations requires distinguishing between transhistoricism and diachrony. Though both concepts are concerned with long-term connections and divisions, the two differ in their attitudes to both periodization and teleology. Diachronic approaches have been adopted in classics from Ferdinand de Saussure's *Cours de linguistique générale*. In Saussurean linguistics, the concepts of synchrony and diachrony are used to characterize the evolutionary processes of language. Saussure defined synchrony as "a length of time" (*un espace de temps*) of minimal linguistic change, be it a decade, a generation, or a century, and he compares it to "periods" in political history: "a historian talks about the 'Antonine age' or the 'age of Crusades,' when he takes into account a group of characteristics which remained consistent during that time."[45] Criticisms of Saussure's methodology have observed that language, like other cultural forms, never experiences true fixity and that the pursuit of synchrony obscures variations that aid interpretation. Others have noted that his method privileges periods of literary production, whose constituent grammars are those of the educated elite. These and other critiques are elaborated in the interdisciplinary collection of essays on diachrony edited by José M. González.[46] Snodgrass' contribution to the volume on the history of critical approaches to ancient Greek agriculture shows the danger of supplementing ancient sources with data extrapolated from contemporary ethnographies.[47] In critiquing the narratives of fixity (synchrony) in agricultural practice, Snodgrass uses archaeological evidence (the Boeotia Survey) to argue for long-term diachronic change in Greek agriculture. His concept of diachrony interrelates ancient with modern agricultural practices and is framed in the traditional periodization scheme of Greek history (Archaic/Classical/Hellenistic) that Snodgrass realizes does not fit the evidence:

> the intensive surveys brought to light a scatter of small locations, with dense deposition of pottery and other datable finds showing that some kind of concentrated activity (if not necessarily permanent habitation) had taken place there in the classical period. In some cases, this distribution could be shown to have started during the preceding Archaic phase; more often, it could be shown to have continued to prevail into the early part of the ensuing Hellenistic age; nearly as often, the same locations were occupied at other periods, sometimes at a great distance in time.[48]

The author's discomfort with these periodic labels is reflected in their shifting labels: the classical is a "period," the archaic a "phase," and the Hellenistic an "age." The valuable point being made implicitly is how periodization confuses our understanding of hyperlocal practices (agricultural, in this case). Because Saussurean diachrony relies on the existence of independent lengths of time (*espaces de temps*), it will never be free from the problems of periodization. While diachronic studies accept the reality of discrete evolutionary periods as the fundamental analytical units of historical linguistic research, transhistorical studies emphasize processes and temporalities that transcend periodization.

If historical models that look for precipitous social change in moments of disruption omit enduring structures and long-term processes, but models that look for continuities devalue the transformative potential of particular events in specific places, where does that leave us? Davies frames the problem as "interweaving different narratives in different theatres in such a way as to show both their interdependence and their degrees of interlocking."[49]

60 Transhistorical

One lesson that emerges from the study of transregional geographies and multicultural places is how periodization shapes our investigation of the past by conditioning our expectations and our understandings of place. Time and place are always closely intertwined, but not always in obvious ways. Davies' observations reveal the cultural and political forces that shape our view of antiquity, but they also reveal alternative possibilities. One is the decentering movement described in the last chapter as part of the globalization scholar's toolkit, which in this instance would *re*-center parts of ancient Greek history as tangential to the history of Persia. Another involves the recognition that different categories of ancient history (in this case, politicomilitary history) possess temporalities and chronologies of their own. In his theory of history, Braudel also argued against linear time in historiography and posited three scales for measuring time, each conducive to the study of different forms of history: the *longue durée*, operating at the scale of environmental change; social history, operating at the scale of cultural groups and polities; and individual time, which Braudel called "the history of events" (*événementielle*).[50] These three temporalities are recognizable in the three main temporal perspectives on globalization: the *longue durée* perspective of history, archaeology, and anthropology, which focuses on long-term connectivity and forms of social cooperation (like trade routes and urbanization); the intermediate perspective of sociology and political economy, which attends to the dynamics of modernity and the evolution of world-systems and markets; and the near-term perspective of economics, cultural studies, and political science, which focuses on technologies of production, value and supply chains, and cultural flows.[51] To these temporalities we may now also add the scales of deep history, which extends into the paleolithic, and big history, which embeds globalization in planetary processes operating at the level of cosmic evolution from the Big Bang.[52]

Invoking Braudel does not mean accepting his scheme as a whole or rejecting the practice of periodization altogether. But one benefit of transhistoricism as a complement to diachrony is the reminder that alternative periodizations are possible. Transhistorical approaches seek out alternative temporalities that allow us to make connections between texts, objects, ideas, and events outside the linear flow of homogenous time. They contend that the sharp boundaries often drawn and uncritically accepted between historical periods are always fluid and at times wholly illusory. In recognizing various methods of accounting for time in writing history, we appreciate that historical events, texts, and artifacts may be understood not only within local intervals but also as parts of an imagined past and a future that is constantly being constructed and reconstructed. Global systems and processes like inequality, migration, and conflict play key destabilizing roles at times of social change, but these categories are not universal constants. They manifest themselves in each instance in unique ways that cannot be completely assessed or accurately measured. The disjunctive flows between these processes and periods are reflected in social transformations that appear isolated and confined to ancient contexts but are in fact anything but ancient. The practice of periodization in history sorts and arranges the moments and events of the past together into groups through complex processes of selection and combination. Nevertheless, transhistoricism is not a modality intended to eradicate the practice of periodization from historiography, but rather one by which scholars interested in both continuities and divergences may supplement and fill the gaps left by available periodization schemes. This form of multidimensional historicism studies the relationships between historical scales. Scholars operating in this mode investigate, for instance, how long-term global processes and systems respond to the local pressures and stimuli of the history of events and how these interactions produce social transformations, reflected in the lived experiences of peoples and polities. Transhistoricism as a mode of historical research builds on the analogy with globalization in looking for processes that overflow boundaries, in this case, between periods as well as for alternative modes of perceiving and recording the past. This fluidity among the events and periods in history is analogous to the fluidity of globalizing processes across borders. The pursuit of a transhistorical mode of investigation and analysis means looking for the interconnected or disjunctive relationships that transcend scales of historical analysis.

Establishment of continuities between periods produces alternatives to established schemes of periodization. They facilitate thinking about long-term connections and disruptions beyond periodic borders as well as about alternative, local cultural microhistories that complement (and occasionally subvert) the global macrohistories of the ancient world.[53] Transhistorical thinking is therefore both an empirical and a theoretical challenge. As an empirical challenge, it involves imagining new hybrid data sets that connect evidence from diverse scales of historical investigation (such as the *longue durée*, social history, deep history, and big history). As a theoretical challenge, it involves exploring the assumptions, conditions, and expectations that govern the practice of periodization. The historians of the nineteenth century found in ancient Hellas the break with tradition and the creation of a culturally clean slate needed to sustain a particular image of early European history. By the same token, many among the current generation of scholars find forms of interconnectedness that speak to a globalizing present.

Tradition, reception, and beyond

Globalizing classics involves questioning inherited disciplinary frameworks that divide antiquity into privileged regions and periods and separate antiquity from modernity. One of the cruelest paradoxes and injustices of modernity in my estimation is that it excludes many inhabitants of the present, while including many inhabitants of the past. We have seen how rural Greek farmers of the present day were denied coevalness by contemporary ethnographers who saw them as *"fossilized* relics of ancient Greek culture."[54] Meanwhile Euripides, the tragic poet of the fifth century BCE, has been characterized as modern. W. H. Salter argued that Euripides' "modern" qualities reside in "an extraordinary and unique parallelism" between fifth century BCE Greece and his own day, to the point that "we feel a kinship for the men of this period which we do not feel for the men of other and even fairly recent periods."[55] Salter recognized in Euripides's outlook from the end of the fifth century BCE ("the point at which the synthesis of Hellenic civilization begins to break down") a *fin de siècle* mentality that reflected his own time's anxieties about imperialism and the rivalries of European nations.

Such questions about the shifting attitudes toward ancient ideas, texts, and artifacts and about the history of engagement with them are the province of two related subfields in classical studies: reception studies and the study of the classical tradition. These two methodologies address the histories of adaptation, imitation, and appropriation of classical sources, as well as their changing roles in education, scholarship, and public life. Both strands of classical studies have drawn from developments in critical theory and made claims to reflect a more global approach to classics. This section offers a broad synthesis of the two fields with an emphasis on their similarities and differences, their efforts to globalize the discipline, and what work still remains to be done.

I begin with the classical tradition. Salter's concern to defend the unity of European culture in response to national rivalries is also reflected in T. S. Eliot's influential essay, "Tradition and the Individual Talent." Eliot defined "tradition" as a continuum, an aggregate of all previous creative achievement, out of which an individual artist creates something new. An aspiring poet can perceive and contribute to the tradition only after developing a diachronic awareness that Eliot calls "the historical sense:"

> the historical sense involves a perception, not only of the pastness of the past, but of its presence; the historical sense compels a man to write not merely with his own generation in his bones, but with a feeling that the whole of the literature of Europe from Homer and within it the whole of the literature of his own country has a simultaneous existence and composes a simultaneous order.[56]

Eliot's definition of tradition rejected the view that the measure of a poet's greatness lay in the degree of *departure* from the works of the past. The essay challenged the agonistic model of literary innovation, which set the old against the new and was characteristic of the quarrel of the ancient and the moderns, a debate that had framed discussions of European art and literature since the Renaissance. Instead, Eliot proposed that the work of a great poet reflects not a conflict but a *subordination* of her own mind to "the mind of Europe," which she has learned through study to be more important. Eliot's idea of the "mind of Europe" was influenced by his visit to the Font-de-Gaume cave at Périgueux in August 1919, where he saw the famous wall paintings dating from 17,000 BCE and conceived the idea of a cultural singularity: "which abandons nothing *en route*, which does not superannuate either Shakespeare, or Homer, or the rock drawing of the Magdalenian draughtsmen."[57] This cumulative nature of tradition is one of its essential features. Several characteristics of Eliot's formulation of tradition have become persistent features of the classical tradition: its linear, forward movement through time (e.g., "*from* Homer") and its aggregative mode ("the conception of poetry as a living whole of all the poetry that has ever been written").[58]

Gilbert Murray, whose writings inspired Salter (quoted previously) to read and study Euripides, introduced the concept of "tradition" with the following anecdote:

> Some seventy years ago, a traveler in the Australian bush, riding up at nightfall to a solitary wooden cabin in the district between the Murray and Murrumbidgee rivers, would have found the owner sitting alone at a rough and frugal dinner, in complete evening dress. He wore evening dress for the sake of its associations, because he and his people had done so at home. It was to him part of a tradition of thought and conduct and social atmosphere which he valued and which he felt himself to be in danger of losing. He wore it with emphasis and deliberately, though it was, in his present circumstances, a habit both unusual and inconvenient.[59]

This richly imagined vignette takes place at a juncture where the old flows into the new. The confluence of the two rivers (one named in Wiradjuri, an Indigenous language, the other named to honor Sir George Murray, British Secretary of State for War and the Colonies) contrasts indigeneity with colonialism, with the former (the Murrumbidgee, a tributary) flowing into the latter (the Murray, a main). In his clothes and haircut, accent and manners, habits of thought and conduct, the man dining in evening dress in the Australian outback is a curiosity, an "exotic anachronism" to borrow one of Loring Danforth's memorable phrases. Unlike the Greek farmer, whom this phrase describes in Danforth's critique of anthropological discourse,

64 Transhistorical

Murray's traditionalist is not denied coevalness but conscientiously rejects aspects of the present through his embodiment and performance of an imagined and idealized past. In Murray's sincere, almost naive words, "The tradition represented a memory which he loved and was proud of, and to which he intended to be true."[60] The love of this memory, idealized though it may be, makes the traditionalist a stranger both in time and in place. One might even call him a colonist, who experiences the present as an explorer does, never losing sight of where he is originally from.

Nearly a half-century after Murray's imaginative, Australian vignette Robert Bolgar also characterized the classical tradition in terms of exploration and colonialism. Here is Bolgar's description of the labor of accounting "our debt to Greece and Rome:"

> After centuries of effort—fifteen centuries as a matter of fact—we see ourselves still at the primitive stage of discovery, where the unexplored ground before us is so vast that we can do no more than just probe it at random. Like early travelers in Africa, we are familiar with a stretch of coastline here, a river there, but the overall plan of our continent is hidden from us.[61]

Bolgar was one of several scholars during the twentieth century's two postwar periods, also including Gilbert Highet, who gave shape to the study of the classical tradition by tracing the history of classical learning from the end of antiquity into modern Europe.[62] These scholars viewed the histories of survival and transmission as the preservation of an ancient literary and philosophical heritage, bequeathed to and resuscitated by those who possessed the necessary learning and disposition. This conception of the classical tradition was sustained by the notion that the ancient culture demanded keen and educated minds to reanimate it. Highet's book claimed that:

> Great systems of thought, profound and skillful works of art, do not perish unless their material vehicle is utterly destroyed. They do not become fossils, because a fossil is lifeless and cannot reproduce itself. But they, whenever they find a mind to receive them, live again in it and make it live more fully.[63]

Because the classical past was dead, complete, and finished, its rules and lessons were established, fixed, and unchanging.[64]

Drawn from the world of intergenerational finance and inherited wealth (familiar to the European upper classes), metaphors of value, legacy, inheritance, and debt became the most popular vehicles for positioning the cultures of modern, "Western" Europe as the heirs to the ancient Greek and

Roman past. The "debt" owed to Greece and Rome framed the collections of essays by R. W. Livingstone (1921) and Cyril Bailey (1924), as well as the series of over forty volumes edited between 1922 and 1948 by Hadzsits and Robinson and entitled, *Our Debt to Greece and Rome*.[65] Highet's book opened with the claims that "Our world is the direct spiritual descendant of Greece and Rome" and "in most of our intellectual and spiritual activities we are the grandsons of the Romans, and the great-grandsons of the Greeks."[66] The "we," whom Highet addresses as cobeneficiaries in this inheritance, are the authors and audiences of English, French, German, and Italian literature, precisely the major European combatants of the Second World War. The reanimation of a shared European past might soothe open wounds, and so Highet framed the study of the classical tradition as the influential source of national European literary histories. The text is structured as a chronological survey of classical learning through the major cultural centers and periods of Western European history, beginning with the Dark Ages, about which I have said enough for the moment. Profoundly influenced by Werner Jaeger's thesis that civilization progressed not through power and wealth but through education, Highet's book drew heavily on Livingstone's and Bailey's collections, as well as on national histories of English, German, and French literature.[67] These early studies in the classical tradition gave ideological legitimacy to European institutions, beliefs, and values.[68] Their narratives and arguments are predicated on a belief not only in the historical and cultural continuity between the ancient world and that of their own elite, learned, European societies but also in their preeminence over other cultures, both ancient and modern. By emphasizing the debts owed to these ancient cultures, whose influence might be clearly observed in many facets of contemporary cultural life, early studies of the classical tradition sought to legitimize the social and cultural practices of the Anglo-American upper classes.

The heroes of Highet's narrative were the great minds of European literary history. He announced unapologetically that his book would deal "only with literature, and will refer to other fields of life only to illustrate important literary events."[69] The conflation of the study of antiquity with the study of its literature is characteristic of scholarship of the nineteenth and early twentieth centuries.[70] This tendency is evident in Bolgar's edited proceedings of a 1969 conference featuring two papers on classical influences in architecture, four papers on manuscript traditions, and twenty-one papers on literary and philosophical subjects.[71] These studies privileged selected, canonical texts reflecting an imagined elite experience of antiquity and implied that only those with specialized knowledge of these texts had access to their wisdom. Even in parts of the field today, the notion endures that ancient authors like Thucydides wrote deliberately difficult texts that were intended "ONLY for the elite, not for the common person."[72] This notion of a great chain of influence linking the great literary minds of the Greeks and Romans to their counterparts in the Renaissance, Enlightenment, Victorian, and Modern periods has largely been abandoned, as historians have gradually given up the study of literary history as a progression of influences.[73]

Because of the role of classical education (the context in which the tradition was guarded and transmitted) in shaping European cultural and political (including colonial) elites, the collapse of empires and the struggles for political independence in the period following the Second World War posed significant challenges to the study of classics. No academic discourse so steeped in cultural imperialism and the logic of colonialism (as in Murray's and Bolgar's characterizations of the classical tradition) could escape being perceived as neocolonialist. As a result, in the intervening years, study of the classical tradition has evolved in response to decolonization, postcolonialism, and the development of critical theory and has attempted to distinguish itself from studies in classical receptions, which have emerged during the same period. The reanimated form of the classical tradition involves the pursuit of holistic treatments of traditions of classical learning (still defined as ancient Greek and Roman) around the world. In his introduction to the 2007 *Companion to the Classical Tradition*, Craig Kallendorf characterizes the historical approach of the classical tradition as a "chain of receptions," a linear and coherent narrative linking successive readings of texts and objects through time.[74] Another recent study, by Michael Silk, Ingo Gildenhard, and Rosemary Barrow, defines the field in terms of "what is sometimes skeptically referred to as the grand sweep or the big picture."[75] The pursuit of a holistic, diachronic account of classical learning remains a significant ideological and rhetorical difference between the study of the classical tradition and studies of classical receptions, to which we will turn now.[76]

Since the 1990s, classical reception studies has developed into a major field of research in classics. This methodology emerged from developments in critical theory and from dissatisfaction with the classical tradition, which as we have seen, used concepts of legacy and influence to describe the transmission and dissemination of culture through the ages. Classical reception studies draw instead from reader response theories by Hans Robert Jauss and Wolfgang Iser, who posited that reading was itself a creative act commensurate with writing. Jauss' theory of reception presented an alternative to Marxist and formalist modes of literary interpretation focused on the system of production and the mechanics of representation. These schools of criticism, he argued, omitted the reader/listener/spectator in the production of meaning: "History of literature is a process of aesthetic reception and production which take place in realization of literary texts on the part of the receptive reader, the reflective critic and the author in his continued creativity."[77] This dialectic was reframed by Iser as the two "poles" of the literary work, the artistic and the aesthetic, that frame the actualization of the work. "If the virtual position of the work is between text and reader," he explained, "its actualization is clearly the result of an interaction between the two, and so exclusive concentration on either the author's techniques or the reader's psychology will tell us little about the reading process itself."[78] Building on these theories of reader response, the field of classical receptions explores the contexts in which ancient Greek and Roman artifacts have been appropriated, adapted, portrayed, or otherwise "received" through time, including in antiquity.[79] The fruitful possibility of reading classical receptions in antiquity is one way that the classical tradition, defined as postclassical, is sometimes thought to differ from reception studies.[80]

Among the first to apply this approach was Charles Martindale, whose book from 1993, *Redeeming the Text*, challenged the positivism of Latin literary studies. Rather than seeing a text's meaning as accessible through scientific methods of analysis, Martindale argued that meaning emerged from a dialectic of text and reader: "our current interpretation of ancient texts, whether or not we are aware of it, is in complex ways, constructed by the chain of receptions through which their continued readability has been effected."[81] Another pioneering thinker in classical receptions, Lorna Hardwick, positioned the emerging field even more directly in contrast to studies of the classical tradition in two ways: first, in discarding the language of inherited wealth (legacy, inheritance, debt, heritage), by which the classical tradition implied that the ancient culture was dead and could only be reanimated by a properly educated heir, and second, in acknowledging the diversity of ancient culture and the plurality of possible readings of ancient works, in contrast to the tacit assumption in many studies of the classical tradition that a work's meaning was stable and unproblematic.[82] In this way, studies in classical reception are often closely aligned with feminist and postcolonial readings, which also stress diversity, contingency, obliquity, and hybridity.[83]

These two closely related subfields connect with the study of globalization in distinct ways. The study of the classical tradition offers a model of writing large-scale historical accounts linking the transformations of classical sources through time and making diachronic connections between artifacts that are independent of any direct influence or single, clear original.[84] Reception studies produce transhistorical and multicultural histories of ancient texts and raise ethical questions about the mechanisms for their preservation and transmission, about who is and is not allowed access to them, and about how their meaning is generated. The fact that ancient Greek dramas, for instance, have been adapted and performed at different times as poetry of imperial approbation *and* of political dissent in ancient Rome, as Nazi propaganda, as postcolonial, emancipatory texts in Latin America, as myths of liberation and reconciliation in sub-Saharan Africa, as an allegory for migrants and refugees in Syria, and to comfort and give meaning to the experience of combat veterans in the United States (and in hundreds of other places and times) vividly attests to the transcultural, transhistorical value of classical reception studies. A chief aim of both methodologies is to document and analyze what classics and classical learning have come to mean in the postcolonial world. By linking the postclassical history of ancient texts with the modern history of ideas, they have catalyzed research that might very well be described as global in its scope and aims, yet both methodologies remain rooted in a national imaginary of fixed borders, within which global and international are synonymous. That is, they are constrained within the bounds and imaginative frameworks of the modern system of nations. A common approach involves the accumulation and analysis of traditional periods and distinct places, which are commonly modern territorially bounded states. Because national identities are largely predicated on shared linguistic heritage, literary histories are still very often national literary histories, as reflected in treatments of the subject by Highet and Bolgar in the 1940s and 1950s. Highet's delineation of the classical tradition adopted a nationalistic outlook, as we have seen, from literary histories in English, German, Italian, and French. The same methodological nationalism is reflected in Kallendorf's *Companion to the Classical Tradition*, which divides its subject explicitly into "Periods" and "Places" reflecting traditional periodizations of modern European history and emphasize European nations.

Studies in the classical tradition in particular demonstrate this outlook by continuing to place the cultural history of the "West" at the center of their narratives (whether explicitly or implicitly) and continuing to adopt a value-oriented language that borders on canon formation. The *International Journal of the Classical Tradition* opened its inaugural issue in 1994 with an exploratory essay by George Kennedy that offered an introductory chronology of the reception of Hellenism. The paper attempts to situate the classical alongside other "Western" discourses (including Christianity, Judaism, science, capitalism, Marxism, feminism, and multiculturalism), "to which society and thinkers have turned in many of the critical points of cultural history and from which they have borrowed freely."[85] Kennedy's chronology unfolds as a series of (fifteen) Hellenizations, first in the Near East, Egypt, and Rome and then in moments in postclassical history when influential thinkers and authors embraced classical learning: Pope Gregory I, Averroes, Machiavelli, Luther, Melanchthon, and Milton, Corneille and Racine, Goethe and Shelley, Tolstoy and Clemenceau, Gide, Cocteau, Anouilh, Sartre, and Giraudoux, and more. The same Eurocentric orientation of the classical tradition is evident in the most recent large-scale treatments of the classical tradition. As we have seen, Kallendorf's *Companion to the Classical Tradition* reproduces Highet's outlook in its adoption of the traditional periodic and nationalist-geopolitical framework.[86] The volume's regional approach is most obviously dependent on a national imaginary, which puts European nations at the center of eight individual chapters. France, Germany, Spain and Portugal, Italy, the Netherlands, Scandinavia, the U.K., and the U.S.A receive separate treatments, while the global south is apportioned two chapters, one covering the whole African continent and the other Latin America. No Asian country is discussed at all. In like manner, the 2014 volume on *The Classical Tradition* by Silk, Gildenhard, and Barrow embraces its Eurocentrism, even while asserting the global nature of the subject:

> The classical tradition at its widest is a global phenomenon (witness Gandhi on Plato, Roman influences on the architecture of the mosque, the Greek-tragic evocations of the plays of Soyinka); and it has certainly been in constant dialogue with other cultural traditions throughout its history; but our discussion is concentrated on Western culture and, within Western culture, on the primary and closely related cultural traditions of Italy, France, Germany, and the English-speaking world.[87]

These are the same national literary traditions emphasized by Gilbert Highet over 70 years ago. The volume mentions Africa and China in a few isolated passages, and Latin America is not mentioned, although in the notes following the passage just quoted the authors confess that Spain and the Hispanic world are their "most significant omission." In one telling instance, the description of Art Deco style contrasts "echoes of the classical" with "decorative motifs from world cultures—African, Chinese, Meso-American," with the clear implication that world cultures are not classical cultures.[88] The authors justify these exclusions in terms of their search for "coherence" within the "undoubted heartland" of the classical tradition, by which they clearly mean western Europe. Citing a comment by Femi Osofisan, a Nigerian playwright, that his adaptation of Euripides' *Trojan Women* was written with a Nigerian audience in mind, Silk, Gildenhard, and Barrow note that "Euripides 'reclaimed' as 'world literature' is different from Euripides as part of the Western classical tradition."[89] Because of the continued reliance on national literary and cultural histories, practitioners of these methods have only begun to consider and theorize the remains of ancient cultures in transnational terms.

Scholars of classical receptions are not immune to methodological nationalism. Like scholars of the classical tradition, researchers in reception studies often view the globe as a collection of territorially bounded nations each containing isolated and fixed traditions and texts, whose links in the chain of receptions are separate from those of other national traditions. Theorizing about the role of the transhistorical in reception studies draws attention to the competing temporalities that frame the views of the past from the perspective of the present. Martindale describes how reception,

> operates with a different temporality, involving the active participation of readers (including readers who are themselves creative artists) in a two-way process, backward as well as forward, in which the present and past are in dialogue with each other.[90]

This multidirectional, aperiodic approach encapsulates reception studies' transhistorical mode. Reflecting on the twentieth anniversary of *Redeeming the Text*, Martindale refined his theory of "the transhistorical" as "the seeking out of often fugitive human communalities across history."[91] This formulation is helpful in making a clearer distinction between tradition and reception. These two subfields of classical studies reflect contrasting temporalities: one linear and diachronic, the other discontinuous and transhistorical. They differ from one another in their orientation to the past and in their ways of thinking about the remains and revivals of antiquity today. The study of the classical tradition operates *diachronically* by tracing a single, long chain of receptions through time to its origins in the past. Its logic is diachronic because it accepts (and in fact depends on) clearly defined periods, which can then be bridged by history and tradition.[92] Even while acknowledging that no account of influences will ever be truly comprehensive, studies in this vein nevertheless aim to craft a linear narrative, originating in antiquity and enduring through a chain of ensuing readings, which, accumulated over time, constitute the tradition. As a result, though there may be many links in the chain of receptions, the chain itself is generally thought of as whole, unified, and singular.

By contrast, the study of classical receptions operates *transhistorically* through a logic that is discontinuous and focused not on the chain, but on the links. Classical reception studies eschew questions of origin and value, and for this reason they are often perceived as relativistic.[93] The methodology's utility lies in decentering the ancient original by imagining receptions as complex hybrids. In further contrast to studies in the classical tradition, work on classical receptions envisions transhistorical relationships as mutually constitutive. It conceives of the remains of the past not as a single, carefully wrought and lovingly preserved chain of texts and ideas but as a complex, relational network of sources, whose meanings are often contingent on the responses of other members in the network, including later recipients.[94] Nevertheless, as a result of this orientation, studies in classical receptions struggle to address instances of hybrid receptions that lack clear

Transhistorical 71

originals and to combine multiple receptions coherently into the sorts of interconnected, diachronic narratives that the classical tradition is designed to produce. For this reason, both methodologies aid in developing a global classics that is sensitive to transhistorical, cultural flows at multiple levels of historical analysis and can construct and integrate local micronarratives with global macronarratives.

As we have seen, it is vital to reflect on contrasting methods for measuring, recording, and narrating the events of the past whenever considering questions of long-term global change. The linear, diachronic narrative of the classical tradition, as developed in the early twentieth century, embraces a linear, cumulative narrative mode and the homogenizing logic of colonialism, while the discontinuous, transhistorical narratives of classical receptions draw instead from feminist and postcolonial theories that stress "not homogeneity but conflicts and discontinuities."[95] These divergent scholarly narratives reveal the implicit modernist and postmodernist backgrounds of globalization narratives: some characterize globalization in terms of forward progress, inevitability, and the erasure of difference, while others see globalization in terms of diverse, multidirectional processes that produce distinct forms of local culture. By exploring the alternative temporalities of diachronic tradition versus transhistorical reception, we can appreciate how these distinct narratives reflect the ways that generations of readers and scholars have related to the global past.

Conclusion: multiple antiquities

Transhistoricism is a mode of global historical inquiry that seeks diverse connectivities between people, places, texts, objects, and ideas over vast stretches of time. It is inherently comparative, pursuing connections that transcend established schemes of periodization, even if they do not aim to efface the notion of periodic change altogether. Rather, transhistorical investigation embraces the possibility of multiple parallel, even orthogonal, histories of antiquity that reflect the complex dynamics of human interconnectedness in different realms of experience over time. This transhistorical notion of multiple antiquities represents a view of the remote past that contravenes long-held academic and popular views of classical antiquity. In particular, it contests the view, prevalent since the eighteenth century, that the civilizations of Greece and Rome possess a unity and coherence, whose individual aspects—even when centuries apart—are interrelated to a degree that is unique in the history of human societies.[96] The founders of the classical discipline all assumed, even if only implicitly, that the cultural unity of antiquity was the feature that distinguished it from modernity and made it a suitable object of historical study. This assumption of unity involves the exclusion of cultural groups (e.g., the Minoans, Mycenaeans, Macedonians), who are denied coevalness on account of their divergent forms of social organization and identity expression.

The denials of coevalness that legitimize Eurocentric and occidentalist accounts of modernity are sustained by the sociotemporal alienation of the classical and medieval worlds. Fabien has pointed out how denial of coevalness with the Middle Ages functions to legitimize Western imperialism, and medievalists have built upon Blumenberg's and Fabien's work by showing the structural importance of the Middle Ages in supporting the ideology of modernity.[97] In response to this ideology, postcolonial critics of periodization in historiography have argued that all temporal categories are mobile. Any society, text, object, or individual that is perceived as not yet modern may at any time be labelled medieval, premodern, ancient, or classical, like the modern Greek farmer characterized by ethnographers as an "exotic anachronism".[98] "Historicism," writes Dipesh Chakrabarty, "came to non-European peoples in the nineteenth century as somebody's way of saying 'not yet' to somebody else."[99] Chakrabarty's critique of historicism builds on Fabian's work to explore temporality in subaltern studies. In his view, the teleological narrative of progress or development inherent in the Eurocentric account of modernization/globalization is a colonizing mechanism, which depends on the narrative of "first in Europe and then elsewhere."[100] The rhetoric of progress and development permits the characterization of life in modern India as a contradictory fusion of multiple historical periods. In one frequently quoted interview, the managing director of Nestle India Ltd., Daraius Ardeshir, remarks that, "Indians are capable of living in several centuries at once," adding, "when I visit my father's house I still kneel and touch my forehead to his feet." Such a characterization is only possible because the speaker has encountered the traditional, Eurocentric periodization of global historical time, which has clearly separated the several centuries into the homogenous narrative of European history.[101]

One of the most important implications of the idea of multiple antiquities is that the cultural programs of the premodern "West" are not the only authentic or legitimate antiquities. This view builds on Eisenstadt's idea of multiple modernities, which attributes the distinct varieties of modernity (e.g., in India or Japan) to the encounter between European modernity and the cultural histories of non-European societies. Such encounters, made possible by globalization, demonstrate the endless capacity for reinterpretation of modernity's cultural program, as newly empowered decolonized nations embrace and reshape the discourse of modernity in their own terms.[102] As Afir Dirlik observes, "the age of 'global modernity', that is the fragmentation of Eurocentric modernity by competing claims to what it means to be modern, is characterised, not by the denial of coevalness but by temporal *contemporaneity*."[103] This awareness of multiple modernities supports the existence of multiple, competing premodernities by which "non-Western" societies may appropriate and redefine the discourse of medievalism or of antiquity to make their own claims to and about the remote past. These multiple antiquities challenge the dichotomy of tradition and modernity that sustains the occidentalist narrative of modernization. Chakrabarty's account of political modernity in South Asia rests on acknowledging the contemporaneity of non-Eurocentric temporalities and the resulting fragmentation of global historical time.

The same politics of global historicism are visible in the contrasting temporalities of tradition and reception: studies in the classical tradition emphasize long-term continuity, while classical reception studies prefer disjointed contemporaneity. The study of the classical tradition is constructed as a literary historicism in the epic mode, attempting to write a diachronic, cumulative account of cultural influence through time. Its aim is a continuous narrative memorializing how the achievement of the past has been heroically preserved and given new life by great minds through the past and into the present. This macronarrative, celebrating an unbroken chain linking great European minds through time and space, springs from the same teleological narratives of universal progress that sustain modern European political discourse. Its temporality is the empty and homogenous time of developmentalist modernization.[104] But it is important to emphasize that the narrative of the classical tradition requires a singularized antiquity. To seek multiple antiquities destabilizes the condition of unity that is the unacknowledged structuring principle of the field. The subalternist pluralization of antiquity is an interruption in which cultural difference ruptures historicist time: "the subaltern fractures from within."[105]

The study of classical receptions embraces this discontinuous mode of global historiography, which characterizes the relationship between present and past in ways that transcend historical periodization, as disjointed, fragmented, and plural. Emerging in part as a postmodern response to the hegemonic macronarratives of the classical tradition, receptions studies pursue focused comparisons between specific texts and objects, whose meanings are never wholly determined at their point of origin. This axiom is one of the "two great truths" that Charles Martindale proposes in his definition of reception as a "new humanism."[106] The other "great truth" is the principle that efforts to change the present require knowledge of the past and that the two are therefore equally important partners in engaging with the modern world. Receptions studies enables scholars to appreciate how the history of classical antiquity and the histories of modernity and globalization are mutually constitutive. Within the master narratives of globalization (especially those that see it as a process of homogenizing westernization), the classical (like the medieval) represents a spatiotemporal baseline:[107] as the cradle of "Western civilization", as a lost golden age of cultural uniformity and worldly innocence, or as a period of imperial conquest and acculturation that foreshadows our own. Most classicists are aware of these narratives, though only scholars of reception can appreciate the variety of uses to which they have been (and continue to be) put. Nevertheless, it will be clear that the genealogy of Eurocentric modernity, upon which many accounts of globalization are based, draws ideological power from the perceived otherness of the premodern.[108] Recognizing the role of periodization in structuring and sustaining colonial power, Chakrabarty highlights the mutual interest of classicists and postcolonial critics in exploring the inability of European narratives and categories of modernity to capture alternative temporalities. As a product of postcolonial, feminist, and subaltern studies, classical receptions challenges the Eurocentric ideas of unity and permanence with counterhegemonic approaches that draw attention to the presences of the past among those marginalized or omitted from mainstream accounts of tradition.[109] In contrast to the classical tradition, reception studies adopts not continuity but *contemporaneity*.

Globalizing antiquity is not therefore *per se* an inclusive enterprise but must resist the homogenizing potential of transnational and transhistorical global discourses reflected in the narrative of the classical tradition. Lisa Lowe and David Lloyd describe the tendency among theorists of transnational global capital "to assume a homogenization of global culture that radically reduces possibilities for the creation of alternatives."[110] Traditional histories of Eurocentric antiquity sustain this assumption by providing a singular point of origin for global modernity that validates a universal teleology in terms of a narrow range of sociopolitical norms (e.g., liberal democracy, citizenship, individual liberty, territorial sovereignty). What is needed in place of this "monoculture of linear time," as Boaventura de Sousa Santos explains, is an "ecology of temporalities" permitting us to recover cultural practices that are unknowable to (and as a result suppressed by) the linear temporality of Eurocentric modernity. "Once these temporalities are recuperated and become known, the practices and socialities ruled by them become intelligible and credible objects of argumentation and political debate."[111] For decades, postcolonial and feminist scholars have been exploring the multiple temporalities that become available by resisting and subverting the teleological narratives of universal progress. Inspired by these efforts, the transhistorical idea of multiple antiquities embraces Chakrabarty's theory of heterotemporality in suggesting that alternative orientations to the remote past coexist with the linear temporality of the classical tradition. Like the idea of multiple globalizations, these multiple antiquities counterbalance historicist macronarratives of globalization from the top down, as an epic poet might have written them, with transhistorical micronarratives of unique risks, dangers, and forms of violence.

Transhistorical 75

The idea of multiple antiquities mirrors the multiple globalizations discussed in the previous chapter, which can be measured and studied at various scales along the global-local spectrum. These complementary narratives of globalization from the bottom up are crucial to the development of a critical ethics for global studies, which in turn makes possible forms of human solidarity that do not depend on universal norms.[112] Imagining what such a critical ethics might mean for the new, global classics is the subject of the next chapter.

Notes

1 For diachrony, see González ed. 2015 and discussion below; transhistoricism in Martindale 2013.
2 Harvey 1989: 293; Cairncross 1997.
3 Steger 2017: 17.
4 Steger and Wahlrab 2017: 53.
5 Momigliano 1966: 181.
6 Horden and Purcell 2000: 77.
7 Birot 1964: 3; Horden and Purcell 2000: 78.
8 Lakoff and Johnson 1980: 41–45; Lakoff and Johnson 1999: Ch. 10; Boroditsky 2000; Casasanto and Boroditsky 2008; Zanker 2019: Ch. 2.
9 Shanks and Tilly 1987; Robb 2007: 9.
10 Lefebvre 1991: 422.
11 Soja 1996: 78.
12 *Ibid.* 81 (ellipsis in original).
13 Robertson 1995: 26.
14 Nederveen Pieterse 2017: 942–94 and *passim*.
15 Flynn and Giráldez 2006.
16 Abu-Lughod 1989.
17 Jennings 2011, 2017.
18 Steger and Wahlrab 2017: 116.
19 *Ibid.* 6
20 Arendt 1958: 270.
21 McLuhan (1964: 6–7 with emphasis added) remarks that, "After three thousand years of specialist explosion and of increasing specialism and alienation in the technological extensions of our bodies, our world has become *compressional* by dramatic reversal. As electrically contracted, *the globe is no more than a village.*"
22 Harvey 2009: 149.
23 Blackbourn 2012.
24 Hayot 2011.
25 For the postmodern critique of periodization in history, see Fulbrook 2002: 18–24; Steger and Wahlrab (2017: 132–137) address the problem of periodization for global studies.
26 Davies 2002; Vlassopoulos 2007: esp. ch. 9; Kotsonas 2016. For a feminist critique of periodization in Roman history, see Hallett 1993.
27 Bintliff 1997.
28 For the impact of Lefkandi, see Antonaccio 1995; Murray 2018: 21–22 and n.25.

29 Murray 2018: 19. As Snodgrass (2000: xxvi) remarks with consternation in his foreword to the reissue of *The Dark Age of Greece*, the terminology that he helped to popularize became an easy target, and few archaeologists specializing in early Greece continue using the term today. Kotsonas 2016: 262.
30 Blumenberg 1983: 115.
31 Cole and Smith 2010: 3.
32 Fabian 2014.
33 Burn 1936: 1; Snodgrass 2000: 22 n.2.
34 Snodgrass 2000 [1971]: 436, and cf. 416–36.
35 Flynn and Giráldez 2006: 211.
36 Shanks and Tilly 1987; Bradley 1991; Lucas 2005.
37 Shanks and Tilly 1987: 119.
38 Fabian 2014 [1983]: 95.
39 The colonization of space and time is not a modern phenomenon, as Paul Kosmin's histories of the Seleucid monarchs (2014, 2018) reveal.
40 Moloney 2015, esp. n.2; Brunt 1976: xxxv; Ellis 1981: 146; Holt 2003: 7–8; Gabriel 2010: 6.
41 Finley 1982 [1954]: 40; Snodgrass 1974: 125; Coldstream 2003 [1977]: 18; Morris 1999: 70; Strauss 2006: 6.
42 For the Cretans, another temporally marginalized group, see Perlman 1998.
43 Snodgrass 2015: 247–28.
44 Danforth 1984: 53.
45 Saussure 1971: 142.
46 González 2015: 5–6.
47 Snodgrass 2015; cf. Danforth 1984.
48 Snodgrass 2015: 355–356.
49 Davies 2002: 228; Vlassopoulos 2007: 208.
50 Braudel 1980: 25–54; Bradley 1991: 209–210; Vlassopoulos 2007: 211–212.
51 Nederveen Pieterse 2017: 938 Table 10.1.2.
52 Christian 2005; Spier 2015; Zinkina et al. 2019.
53 Hallett (1993) offers a feminist critique of periodization in Roman literary studies.
54 Danforth 1984: 53, with emphasis added.
55 Salter 1911: 9–10; Hall and Macintosh 2005: 488–520; Walton 2009: 11–12.
56 Eliot 1932: 14.
57 *Ibid*. 15; on the impact of Eliot's visit to Périgueux, see Bacigalupo 2007.
58 Eliot 1932: 17.
59 Murray 1927: 3.
60 *Ibid*.1927: 5.
61 Bolgar 1971: 1.
62 Bolgar 1973 [1954].
63 Highet 1949: 1. Contrast with the racist description (noted previously) of the Greek peasant as a "fossilized relic" (Danforth 1984: 53).
64 Hardwick 2003: 2; Stray 2007: 6.
65 Livingstone 1921; Bailey 1924; Schein 2008.
66 Highet 1949: 1.
67 *Ibid*. 550–555.
68 Schein 2008.
69 Highet 1949: 2; cf. Rivas Sacconi 1993 [1949].
70 Stray 2007.
71 Bolgar 1973; Stray 2007.

72 Rawlings 2015: 551, emphasis in the original.
73 Hardwick 2003: 2.
74 Kallendorf 2007: 2.
75 Silk, Gildenhard, and Barrow 2014: x.
76 Critiqued in Holmes 2016.
77 Jauss 1970: 10.
78 Iser 1980: 106–107.
79 Martindale 1993, 2006, 2007; Hardwick 2003; Hardwick and Stray 2008.
80 Martindale 2007; Budelmann and Haubold 2008; Silk, Gildenhard, and Barrow 2014: 4–5.
81 Martindale 1993: 7.
82 Hardwick 2003: 2–3.
83 Martindale 1993: 12–13; Hardwick 2007a, 2007b; Zajko 2008.
84 The discussion of the "Dome" in Silk, Gildenhard, and Barrow (2014: 253–262) models their approach to influence-free receptions.
85 G. Kennedy 1994.
86 Highet 1949; Kallendorf ed. 2007.
87 Silk, Gildenhard, and Barrow 2014: 6–7.
88 *Ibid.* 116.
89 *Ibid.* 7 n.13; with critique in Holmes 2016: 277–279.
90 Martindale 2007: 298.
91 Martindale 2013: 173; cf. Holmes 2016: 278.
92 Kallendorf 2007: 2; Silk, Gildenhard, and Barrow 2014: 15–31.
93 Silk, Gildenhard, and Barrow 2014: 5.
94 Butler 2016: 2.
95 Higonnet 1994: 5; Zajko 2008.
96 For a discussion and critique of this view, see Farrell 2019, and the discussion in Chapter 3.
97 Blumenberg 1983; Fabian 2014.
98 Danforth 1984: 53; see preceding discussion.
99 Chakrabarty 2000: 8; cf. Davis 2008: 5; McClure 2015.
100 Chakrabarty 2000: 7–8; with critique in Cheah 2016: 203.
101 Chakrabarty 2000: 48–50.
102 Eisenstadt 2000: 23–24.
103 Dirlik 2007: 94 with emphasis added.
104 Chakrabarty 2000: 15; Davis 2008; 98–100.
105 Chakrabarty 2000: 94; Cheah 2016: 203–204.
106 Martindale 2013: 181.
107 The phrase is from Davis and Altschul 2009: 1.
108 Chakrabarty 2000, 2002; McClure 2015.
109 *Classical Presences* is of course the name of the pioneering series edited for Oxford University Press by two leading practitioners, Lorna Hardwick and James Porter. Cf. Martindale's (2013: 173) "fugitive human communalities across history."
110 Lowe and Lloyd 1997: 1.
111 Santos 2004: 169; Cheah 2016: 12.
112 Albert 1999; Neufeld 2001. For globalization from the bottom up, see Appadurai 2000; della Porta et al. 2006; Nederveen Pieterse 2013: 509.

3 Transdisciplinary

The preceding chapters have explored methodologies within classics that reveal the complexity of the field's engagement with globalization studies over the past few decades and the potential for a sustained dialogue with global studies in the future. This complexity is reflected in the diversity of subfields currently working to globalize the discipline in various ways. Some scholars, drawing from models of globalization developed by social scientists, have proposed new ways of understanding the dynamics of cross-border connectivity, mobility, exchange, and identity in antiquity. This work has resulted in the development of innovative models of large-scale social transformation as well as in detailed studies of microhistorical processes using a range of data sets and specializations. Other scholars have focused on global temporalities, challenging traditional ways of collecting the history of events into periods and seeking alternative moments of social and cultural transformation, patterns of continuity on various scales, and methods by which to compare processes operating across these scales. Scholars have sought to decolonize the field by pursuing the study of classical traditions and receptions throughout the postcolonial world. Without a doubt, this growing body of scholarship constitutes the beginning of a global turn in classics, and it is precisely the *complexity* of this field-wide project that is the subject of this chapter.

Because they play out across many realms of lived experience and human activity, global issues cannot be understood from the perspective of a single discipline or methodological approach. In the words of Jan Nederveen Pieterse, global studies is "interdisciplinary, combines diverse databases, and seeks to provide kaleidoscopic and panoramic perspectives on global conditions and cognitions."[1] The dynamics of cross-border, transhistorical interconnectedness produces problems (both acute and chronic) in social well-being, including war, imperialism, colonialism, piracy, poverty, inequality, enslavement, migration, urbanization, cultural bias, and disease, that operate in many dimensions of life and are reflected in many different kinds of sources, including both objects and texts. But addressing global processes and issues transhistorically from multidisciplinary perspectives and using diverse data sets looks uncomfortably close to a universalism that erases differences and emphasizes uniformities. The study of all human things everywhere and always is not a serious disciplinary mandate. The global turn from interpretive modes based on bounded regional entities and disjointed periods to others based on complex forms of interconnectivity requires a disciplinary reorientation as well.

This chapter undertakes a comparative epistemology of global studies and classics, with particular focus on those parts of the field working to globalize the discipline. The study of global issues transcends disciplinary boundaries and traditional arrangements of academic knowledge, in the same way that the issues themselves transcend time and place. As Manfred Steger puts it:

> Multidimensional processes of globalization and their associated global challenges such as climate change, pandemics, terrorism, digital technologies, marketization, migration, urbanization, and human rights reflect examples of transnational issues that both cut across and reach beyond conventional disciplinary boundaries.[2]

But the predominant structures of modern universities compartmentalize knowledge in ways that are over a century old. While the study of global issues is not new to scholars of antiquity, most teaching and research continue to take place within specializations that, despite the field's transdisciplinary history, mirror the rest of the university. That we recognize, appreciate, and embrace that transdisciplinary history is critical in advancing debates and theories about global classics. Because global studies embraces transdisciplinarity as a founding principle, classics' long-established model for transdisciplinarity makes the two fields ideal interlocutors. A reorientation of the field around problems of social well-being, informed as appropriate by theories of globalization and adopting a transhistorical outlook, will facilitate new kinds of investigation and generate new forms of knowledge. These in turn will reinforce the public roles of classics and classicists in addressing contemporary global issues.

Holism, ecumenicism, and the global

Global studies has developed over the last decade as a deliberately transdisciplinary project, which views with skepticism the fracturing and fragmentation of human lived experience into narrowly conceived areas of specialized knowledge. It has been observed in fact that faculty are often attracted to programs in global studies on account of this deeply held skepticism.[3] Programmatic accounts of the field frequently emphasize its interdisciplinary character. Nederveen Pieterse's distinction between studies in globalization and global studies is grounded in a critique of disciplinary perspectives on questions of global social change, which are driven by the conventions, social demands, technical language, and theoretical underpinnings of distinct disciplines.[4] Steger and Wahlrab make transdisciplinarity one of their "four pillars" of global studies, summarizing the four major dynamics of transdisciplinarity as follows: the systematic integration of knowledge, the transgression of disciplinary boundaries, the pursuit of holistic frameworks, and "an issue-driven focus on problem-solving in the life-world that elevates concrete research questions and practices over disciplinary concerns."[5] Likewise, Darian-Smith and McCarty devote an entire chapter to the limitations of traditional disciplines in exploring complex global issues.[6] Their "global transdisciplinary framework" facilitates the holistic study of multidimensional global issues, while including alternative perspectives and epistemologies in the production of knowledge about globalization. My approach to the subject throughout this chapter is heavily indebted to these discussions.

Since its first formulation in the 1970s, interdisciplinarity has become perhaps the most popular and abused term in the English-speaking academic world—though global is nowadays not far behind. Interdisciplinary studies have grown in response to dissatisfaction with the heavily patrolled and rigid boundaries of disciplines, a concept with a long and complex intellectual history. Long before "discipline" denoted the individual branches of knowledge that constitute modern systems of education and training, Roman soldiers worshipped at altars of *Disciplina*, who reflected their virtues of severity, frugality, self-mastery, and loyalty. Several of these inscribed altars have been found at the extremities of the Roman world. One from the site of the Roman fort at Birrens in Dumfriesshire, Scotland, for instance, is dedicated "To the *Discipline* of the Emperor by the Second Cohort of Tungrians."[7] A similar dedication has been found at a Roman camp in North Africa.[8] The modern term discipline has both etymological and philosophical links to premodern ways of organizing knowledge and structuring pedagogical relations, and many theorists therefore explicitly root the concept of discipline in antiquity. Nevertheless, the modern ordering of scientific knowledge to be taught is a product of nineteenth century European universities, whose academic fields and categories have come to shape global higher education. The French philosopher of deconstruction, Michel Foucault, construed disciplines in terms of their potentially violent methods of controlling human bodies and reducing them to docile relationships of utility.[9] Foucault tied discipline to the needs of the emerging nation-state for bodies capable of undertaking the needed forms of economic, political, and military labor. Disciplines facilitated the creation of a regime in the eighteenth century that appeared egalitarian and representative, but which, through "inegalitarian and asymmetrical systems of micropower called 'disciplines'," guaranteed when necessary the submission of forces and bodies.[10]

In addition to Foucault's biopolitics, however, disciplinarity also constitutes a spatial politics, which operates as the exertion of power over knowledge understood as *terrain*. Spatial metaphors are the most common ways to describe the organization of scientific human knowledge: field, landscape, ecosystem, and sometimes even turf. Besides these, the phrase "boundary work" emerged in the 1980s as a way to describe attempts by scientists to craft a public self-image in which scientific activities could be contrasted with nonscientific activities. In a pioneering study of this phenomenon, which coined the term boundary work, Thomas Gieryn contextualized scientific boundary work within the history of attempts to demarcate science by identifying its unique and essential characteristics. These attempts at demarcation amount to an ideology and a rhetoric through which the intellectual landscape has been broken up over time into allegedly separate institutional and professional fields. But the creation by disciplinary boundary work of differentiated aims, methods, and expertise is, in Gieryn's analysis, only apparent and illusory. Boundary work in scientific literature emerges from his study as an "ideological style" of rhetorical self-presentation that is deployed in three important public-facing contexts:

(a) when the goal is expansion of authority or expertise into domains claimed by other professions or occupations, boundary-work heightens the contrast between rivals in ways flattering to the ideologists' side; (b) when the goal is monopolization of professional authority and resources, boundary-work excludes rivals from within by defining them as outsiders with labels such as "pseudo," "deviant," or "amateur"; (c) when the goal is protection of autonomy over professional activities, boundary-work exempts members from responsibility for consequences of their work by putting the blame on scapegoats from outside.[11]

By showing how boundary work has functioned through time to protect professional autonomy and compete for resources, Gieryn argues that disciplinary definitions and boundaries are flexible, ideological creations, constantly being constructed and reconstructed. When I describe interdisciplinary boundary work as involving a spatial politics, I mean that disciplinary boundary work operates as a form of colonialism, demarcating, appropriating, and occupying territories of investigation and knowledge. From this perspective, disciplines and interdisciplines involve a politics of representation that governs which fields and categories are included or excluded, how they should be grouped together into various configurations, and what their focus and who their audience should be.

While many scholars have turned to interdisciplinary work as offering an escape from the columbaria of their fields and an opportunity to work collaboratively on solutions to complex issues in the "real world," significant anxieties quickly emerged. Often discussions of the virtues of interdisciplinarity assume incorrectly that all disciplines share a level playing field, and as a consequence they neglect to address the considerable asymmetries of power at work in research and collaboration that crosses fields. These asymmetries themselves come in many forms, resulting from years of successful boundary work by various disciplines, especially by scientific disciplines at the expense of nonscientific ones, as described by Gieryn. They include both objective, measurable imbalances in funding opportunities among departments and disciplines and uneven access to and exploitation of labor by postgraduate and postdoctoral students, as well as subjective imbalances in public and institutional perceptions of departmental and disciplinary relevance or prestige. Given the intense competition among departments and programs for limited institutional funding, the establishment and growth of interdisciplinary centers and clusters has strained resources and led to the defunding of existing faculties. This trend is at times mitigated by the growing interest by both public and private funding agencies in supporting interdisciplinary research that addresses "real-world" issues and informs questions of strategy and policy. But external funding solutions risk unduly shaping the direction of research agendas and even careers, with long-lasting effects. Interdisciplinary research and teaching might also be said to weaken existing faculty governance structures by creating supradepartmental structures in the form of centers, programs, and groups that exist outside of established hierarchies. In sum, interdisciplinarity is perhaps best described as a mixed blessing.[12]

In attempting to mitigate these and other concerns, some scholars have seen *transdisciplinarity* as a preferable mode of cross-field research and collaboration. The differences between *inter-*, *multi-*, and *trans*disciplinarity have been much discussed.[13] Alvarogonzález differentiates interdisciplinarity, describing situations of knowledge sharing between disciplines, from transdisciplinarity, which refers to knowledge that "goes over and above disciplinary boundaries following a process that assembles disciplines and recombines information."[14] Its objective is to craft holistic accounts that emphasize dynamics and systems. Julie Thompson Klein produces a four-part typology of transdisciplinarity, including first, systematic knowledge integration; second, holism and the pursuit of synthetic paradigms; third, critical interdisciplinarity and "antidisciplinarity;" and fourth, problem-solving and the need "to frame research questions and practices, not disciplines."[15] Steger and Wahlrab's justification of transdisciplinarity in global studies is predicated on the widespread view that "the study of globalization requires close encounters with multiple forms of complexity and differentiation."[16] The traditional structure and ordering of knowledge in modern academic disciplines lack the tools to analyze globalizing processes that operate unevenly through time and across many domains of human existence and activity. Steger and Wahlrab offer examples of studies of global complexity by scholars in global studies, like Manuel Castells and John Urry, whose explorations of complex forms of interconnectivity embrace transdisciplinarity in order to "combat knowledge fragmentation" and write holistic accounts of shifting dynamics of globalization.[17]

Like other interdisciplinary fields, classics sits uneasily within the strictly bounded landscape of academic knowledge. Departments of Classics and Classical Studies are characterized by a diversity of specializations that is implicitly critical of the fragmented mindset of specialized disciplinary knowledge. In their "very short introduction" to the field, Mary Beard and John Henderson consider that the "most striking" feature of the discipline is "the range of what has been deemed to count as *Classics*, and how boundaries between *Classics* and other disciplines have been defined and re-defined."[18] Nevertheless, the field's *inter*disciplinarity has already been shown to lead to a fragmentation of knowledge about antiquity and the creation of a subdisciplinary landscape that mirrors the larger institutional structures. This process can be observed in the increase of cross-disciplinary traffic among ancient history, archaeology, and the social sciences (especially cultural anthropology), as well as in the emergence of reception studies as a branch of classical scholarship, which has put literary scholars of antiquity into dialogue with departments of modern languages, literatures, and cultures. But as these connections proliferate, others inevitably shrivel. Increases in *inter*disciplinary traffic are often balanced by decreases in *intra*disciplinary traffic, causing gaps between historians, archaeologists, philologists, philosophers, and scholars of reception to grow wider. All of this is easily overstated, but the phenomenon is plain in treatments of globalization and the global. Scholars pursuing a globalizing agenda for the field from within separate, subdisciplinary niches rarely engage with each other's work at all. As a result, little dialogue exists between those globalizing classics through frames drawn from history, archaeology, economics, anthropology, and sociology and those globalizing classics from the perspectives of art, literature, philosophy, and reception. This is true despite the fact that many of these scholars are working within the same transborder, transhistorical modalities, challenging spatiotemporal boundaries from within their niches of the larger field. To appropriate Klein's typology, the utility of transdisciplinary models for classical studies lies precisely in their ability to assemble distinct knowledge sets, their concern with the "big picture," and their attention to problem-solving in the contemporary world. Among several ways to understand the word global in global classics is the field's interest in *completeness*: its aspirations to aggregate and investigate the variety of ancient lifeways and to craft comprehensive, transhistorical accounts linking antiquity to today. Yet despite the obviously transdisciplinary character of the field, few programmatic formulations and defenses of transdisciplinarity exist in classics. A collaborative dialogue with transdisciplinary fields like global studies can spark the development of new multidimensional approaches and multilevel orientations to the remains of antiquity.

Aspects of this transdisciplinary phase of the field's global turn were already in place over two decades ago, when Charles Segal delivered his 1994 presidential address to the (then) American Philological Association. Citing a shift in the field's "center of gravity," Segal celebrated the diversity of classical scholarship, whose junior scholars were "more widely read in anthropology, aesthetics, linguistics, feminist criticism, and literary theory generally, and ... more inclined to experiment with a wide range of methodologies and disciplines."[19] Though sadly he would not live to witness them, Segal correctly anticipated features of the field's global turn, especially the growth of a global consciousness that would decenter European culture within the classical tradition. He offered the following as examples of the "cosmopolitan outlook" of the ancients: the acts of *cosmopoiesis* ("world-making") in Homer's description of Achilles' shield and in Apollonius of Rhodes' description of the ecumene; the processes of lasting social change under the Roman hegemony, as reflected in the notion of *orbi et urbi*, a "great city at the center of the world" (Ovid *Fasti* 2.684); the dynamics of the "local" and the "larger," as he described the relation of Greek literature with Panhellenic culture; and, in particular, the capacity of tragic drama to shift meaning "from the local to the universal" as represented by the figure of Dionysus in Euripides' *Bacchae*, who is characterized simultaneously as foreign, hyperlocal, and universal. These observations of transborder, transcultural features of ancient (literary) culture are consistent with debates about globalization and globality which, though Segal does not mention them, were developing at the time.

Segal's celebration of the field's openness to "many styles of doing Classics" around the world were echoed, nearly 25 years later, in Joseph Farrell's 2019 presidential panel and lecture at the (now) Society for Classical Studies. Farrell's lecture opens with the provocation that the dichotomy of ancient and modern may no longer be the most useful way to frame and legitimize the work of classical scholars. He locates the interdisciplinary origins of classics in the work of German idealist thinkers, who felt strongly that classical civilization was an interrelated whole, all aspects of which were related to one another to a greater degree than in any other historical time or place.[20] In this way, the ancient was crafted as the opposite of the modern, which as we have seen is characterized by fragmentation, discontinuity, and breaks with tradition. As a result of this unique status of classical antiquity, Farrell explains, the classical discipline that emerged was fundamentally different from every other contemporary academic field:

> If you imagine a grid on which the vertical axis is defined by time, with the present at the top, and the horizontal axis is defined by subject areas, with the humanities at one end and the sciences at the other, then all the departments, with their names ranged along the top, would look something like geologists taking a collection of core samples. Each team would find a lot of activity up at the top, near the present, representing courses and research projects in modern literature, modern history, and so forth, and for the most part, they would find less and less activity as the sampling device reached back into earlier, more remote time. *What they would not have, by and large, would be very many lateral connections between different disciplines.*[21]

Farrell's imaginative experiment reveals how knowledge in modern disciplines is organized by subject, place, and time. Disciplines, and the academic departments that claim them, are legitimized by their demarcation of a bounded subject area, within which specialization takes the form of investigating temporal layers within the "core samples" that Farrell describes. The subject area itself is paramount, however, leaving scholars relatively free to find specializations among the layers of the vertical (temporal) axis. Farrell's generalization echoes Eric Hayot's critique of periodization in literary studies, which reveals this organization of knowledge in a neighboring academic field to classics: "our entire system of literary education, from the first-year undergraduate survey to the forms of judgment governing publication, promotion, and tenure, reifies the *period* as its central historical concept."[22] Hayot laments the degree to which the institutionalized expectations of literature departments have remained defined in periodizing terms, despite challenges from schools of critical theory (structuralism, poststructuralism, psychoanalysis, and others) and the development of nonperiodic or transperiodic concepts (genre and subgenre, postcolonial studies, critical race theory, feminism, gender and sexuality studies, etc.).

Classics assumes a contrasting orientation, which Farrell describes as "orthogonal," to the general manner of organizing knowledge in the modern university.[23] Rather than being defined primarily by a subject area, classics embraces the concept of period as its structuring principle, taking as its focus a large, deep stratum of the imagined grid and cutting across the (horizontal) axis of disciplinary subject areas. Most teaching and research in classics departments investigate not the present but a particular slice of the past. Teaching and research take place within a range of subdisciplinary specializations (e.g., language and literature, philosophy, theater, art, architecture, music, religion, political history, economics, etc.) and methodologies (e.g., philology, literary and textual criticism, history, archaeology, linguistics). Because of its orthogonal architecture of knowledge, emphasizing a holistic view of the remote past through a synthesis of many individual, subdisciplinary perspectives, classics departments are fundamentally transdisciplinary entities.

From its German idealist roots, classics developed an unusual orientation of particular to general, by pursuing through its various specializations a holistic understanding of what was perceived to be a single thing, the ancient world. This phrase, which is one of the most common ways to describe in English what classicists study, reflects the success of the German idealist project and the enduring ideology of modernity, whose legitimacy, as we have seen, is sustained by alleging the alterity of other periods (antiquity and the Middle Ages).[24] While Farrell acknowledges that these features allowed classics to endure as a discipline worthy of departmental status, he remarks that it is not difficult to see that the field has outlived its founding rationale. Though the fiction of the unity of classical antiquity endures in many contexts outside of the field, especially in relation to that other popular fiction, "Western civilization", a shrinking number of classicists and ancient historians would care to defend this view. On the contrary, the transdisciplinary diversity of materials and methods within classical studies reflects the plurality of antiquities open to investigation and comparative study. The ancient world is not a single, unified, and coherent entity but rather is constituted and reconstituted as an imaginative fusion of discontinuous and fragmented remains. In understanding this fusion, I have found it helpful to think in terms of what Mikhail Bakhtin called a "chronotope," an artistic construction of time and space in which "spatial and temporal indicators are fused into a concrete whole."[25] In his reading of ancient novels, Bakhtin explains how the characters' adventures take place outside of biological and biographical time in ways that leave the heroes "no less fresh and handsome" at the story's conclusion. In contrast to the novels' transregional plots, which often transport their characters across multiple geopolitical and cultural borders, the events of the ancient novel are "excluded from the kind of real duration in which additions to a normal biography are made."[26] In like manner, the perceived unity and coherence of the ancient world or of classical antiquity are sustained by a creative fusion of places and times (generally speaking, the culture zones of the greater Mediterranean between 1500 BCE and 500 CE).[27] This fusion shares with Bakhtin's reading of the ancient novel the construction through narrative of a unity that emphasizes sameness over difference or (to put it in globalizing terms) homogeneity over heterogeneity. The period logic that constructs classical antiquity as a single entity relies on a narrative of origins, development, peak, decline, supersession, and afterlife that essentializes the modern, Eurocentric worldview with its privileged concepts of originality, innovation, development, belatedness, and decadence.[28]

Farrell's critique of the discipline's origins proposes to dismantle its outdated spatiotemporal frameworks, both its inherited Eurocentrism and occidentalism (space) and its foundational (but artificial) dichotomy of ancient and modern (time). This book has attempted to advance some aspects of this critique. Recognition of the role of the scholarly imagination in constructing ancient worlds invites us to engage in some overdue boundary work. Already a generation ago, Segal noted the role of increasing global consciousness in destabilizing the perceived unity of European culture with the classical as its defining center:

> We are increasingly unsure if European civilization has a center, and at the same time our notions of civilization are becoming less narrowly European. And yet, as some of the great traditional religions narrow into intolerant or irrational fundamentalisms, as values become fragmented and confused in almost every sphere of life, and as profit-driven technology and the mass media gain increasing power, the classical tradition remains as important as ever, and there is still no adequate substitute.[29]

Segal's presidential lecture anticipated by some years the development of classical receptions and globalization theories, which today offer not only adequate but powerful alternatives to the classical tradition as a means of putting the past into dialogue with the present. The transdisciplinary constitution of the field permits forms of transhistorical world-building (*cosmopoiesis*) that are beyond the reach of most academic disciplines, but that are closely matched to the aims and objectives of global studies.[30] In this way, classics aligns with Klein's typology of transdisciplinarity by constructing integrated macronarratives about the remote past and restructuring diverse knowledge sets into new conceptual frameworks.

What about problem-solving in the contemporary world? A core feature of transdisciplinarity missing from these provocations is its concern with addressing problems of lived experience in the present. Klein identifies as a trend line in transdisciplinary studies the core premise that "problems in the *Lebenswelt*—the lifeworld—need to frame research questions and practices, not disciplines."[31] While Segal doubted that classical studies could ever compete for immediacy or relevance with "contemporary-oriented disciplines like sociology or political science or contemporary literature," the field's global turn has generated questions and produced forms of knowledge that rival these disciplines in addressing contemporary problems.[32] The transborder and transhistorical flows that sustain the global study of classics are sensitive to the dialogic relationships among antiquities and modernities, especially those that intersect or conflict with one another.

Toward a critical global classics

As a paradigmatically transdisciplinary field, classics fills a unique niche in the architecture of the arts and sciences by offering models for the multicentric, multiscalar investigation of human societies through history. It has long been understood that the remains of the past contain wisdom by which to understand features of the modern world and vice versa. The work of global classics in challenging the bounded geographies of antiquity and the dichotomy of ancient and modern may open the field to new emphases and perspectives, but it does not fundamentally change our desire to learn from and about the past. Globalization studies helps us to recover and draw attention to the lives, voices, and perspectives omitted from standard accounts that have taken as their focus the urban, male, free, elite, citizen experience. Reception studies encourages us to consider the interconnectivity and transcultural flows of globalization as dynamic, multidirectional processes that flow both forward and backward in time. As a contribution to postcolonialism, these approaches recognize how global identities and cultural expressions are at times embraced and at other times rejected at the local level, reflecting the tension between "cultural homogenization and cultural heterogenization" that Appadurai sees as the fundamental dynamic of globalization.[33]

Inversion of the founding ideologies of classics (e.g., unity and coherence, endurance and permanence) has given the field powerful tools for confronting and decoding the persistent ideologies of modernity. In this way, the field of global classics mirrors the trend among global studies scholars to take socially and politically engaged approaches to their subjects. In their characterization of the socially engaged intellectual, Steger and Wahlrab invoke Pierre Bourdieu's concept of "scholarship with commitment," articulated in his 1999 address to the Modern Language Association in Chicago.[34] Describing the ethical responsibilities of scholars and academics, Bourdieu cited the example of Émile Zola, the French novelist, who challenged his government's unjust conduct during the Dreyfus Affair. Zola exemplified Bourdieu's idea of a "public intellectual" as one who

> engages his specific authority and the values associated with the exercise of his or her craft, such as the values of disinterestedness and truth, in a political struggle—in other words, someone who enters the terrain of politics but without forsaking her exigencies and competencies as a researcher.[35]

In particular, Bourdieu saw the "decisive role" that scholars had to play in resisting "the new neoliberal doxa and the purely formal cosmopolitanism of those obsessed with words such as 'globalization' or 'global competitiveness'." While the engaged public intellectual risks disappointing, even shocking others, Bourdieu urged scholars to break down the "sacred boundary inscribed in their minds . . . between *scholarship* and *commitment*."[36] Early adopters of critical globalization studies expanded Bourdieu's admonitions into the view that, "the exercise of studying the world, of trying to know the world, is itself a social act, committed by agents with a definite relationship to the social order."[37] This provocation by William Robinson encapsulates the consensus that working within the frameworks of globalization obliges scholars to formulate not only theories but critiques of social structures, dynamics, and ideologies. Accordingly, any attempt to theorize a global epistemology for classics should take a critical, socially engaged approach.

Robinson and Richard Appelbaum's foundational overview in *Critical Globalization Studies* forges a link between the field of global studies and the exercise of global justice. The editors understand this project as contributing to the understanding of globalization while at the same time promoting global social justice initiatives:

> We believe that as scholars it is incumbent upon us to explore the relevance of academic research to the burning political issues and social struggles of our epoch, and to the many conflicts, hardships, and hopes bound up with globalization. More directly stated, we are not indifferent observers studying globalization as a sort of detached academic exercise. Rather, we are passionately concerned with the adverse impact of globalization on billions of people as well as on our increasingly stressed planetary ecology. Moreover, we believe that it is our obligation as scholars to place an understanding of the multifaceted

processes of globalization in the service of those individuals and organizations that are dedicated to fighting its harsh edges.[38]

The volume's contributors, including nearly 40 globalization scholars and prominent global social activists, advance this bold agenda. Susan George's opening essay echoes Bourdieu by reiterating the risks that follow the engaged, progressive intellectual and calculating the enormous efforts and expenditures by the reactionary political groups to foster an intellectual climate friendly to their views and policies. In answering the question, "what should be the role and the responsibilities of academia and intellectuals in the global justice movement?" her view is that "critical intellectuals" have a responsibility to make visible the forces and ideological frameworks (including not least their own) behind the production of academic knowledge.[39]

The essays that follow, by William Robinson and James Mittelman, broaden George's injunction into definitions of the field. Robinson identifies critical approaches (in contrast to noncritical) as not accepting the prevailing structures and arrangements of power as natural, and instead problematizing the apparent social and cultural realities:

> What distinguishes (or must distinguish) a critical globalization studies are (1) the subversive nature of its thought in relation to the status quo, and (2) the linkage (actual or attempted) of theory to practice, or the grounding of a critical globalization studies in praxis, in a theoretically-informed practice.[40]

The logic that informs Robinson's critical studies is dialectical and transdisciplinary in bringing different dimensions of human social experience (his examples are race, class, and gender) together in order to understand broader social processes and dynamics. Like George, Robinson explicitly grounds the field in a combination of intellectual and ethicopolitical activity, defending the claim that knowledge of the world is won only through efforts to change it.

Mittelman's definitions of the field also foreground transdisciplinarity and transformative action as its distinguishing features. Mittelman displaces nations and states as the main actors in human events, and instead he recognizes the formation of a polymorphous world produced through the interactions of state-centric and multicentric worlds.[41] This shift in orientation is reflected in the production of knowledge which, especially knowledge about globalization, is rarely produced in isolation of panacademic trends, but results from complex transnational structures and interactions of individual researchers and entities that connect scholars inside and outside of academia through conferences, funding agencies, professional associations, presses, and journals. Because this infrastructure of knowledge production is largely centered in the global north, Mittelman warns that globalization scholars must be self-monitoring: "The critic must listen, remain open, and make ample room for a wide range of voices from various zones, in a vertical and horizontal sense, in the globalization matrix."[42] Building on these questions about the knowledge goals of critical globalization scholars, Mittelman distills five interacting components. The first, *reflexivity*, links knowledge production with material, social, and political contexts, keeping in mind that theories are often (especially in their beginnings) conditioned by their circumstances. The second, *historicism*, acknowledges that globalization describes historical processes that play out through time at varying speeds and in distinct configurations. An understanding of globalization as transhistorical, in ways that avoid treating it as a timeless force operating ahistorically for ever and ever or collapsing it into a feature of some undifferentiated present, requires rigorous historical thinking. The third, *decentering*, responds to globalization's multicentrism by drawing focus away from the attitudes and perspectives of the so-called "West". Because most of the work in globalization studies is produced by scholars in European and North American institutions, critical globalization studies calls for the inclusion of voices, perspectives, and knowledge from outside of these traditional knowledge centers. The fourth, *crossovers*, reflects the importance of transdisciplinary dialogue in studying and addressing global issues. And fifth, *strategic transformations* seek to supplant the dominant "ethos of efficiency, competition, individualism, and consumption" through the counterhegemonic discourse of globalization studies and foster a "new moral order."[43] Taken together, the essays by George, Robinson, and Mittelman offer a robust theoretical framework for the transdisciplinary production of knowledge. Since I have addressed decentering, historicism, and (transdisciplinary) crossovers already, I will focus on reflexivity and transformative practices.

Many common definitions of globalization view it as a process of increasing shared social consciousness. Despite being conceived as shared, this consciousness does not efface differences between local and global identities but fosters a variety of cultural expressions at different levels (local, regional, provincial, global). Cultural reflexivity results from this enhanced awareness of other cultures and identities, for instance, in the diversity of local and regional identities that appropriated and transformed features of Panhellenic or Roman cultures.[44] Critical reflexivity can likewise be understood in terms of awareness and openness to other voices, competing perspectives, and alternative interpretive frameworks. Robinson and Mittelman define reflexivity in terms of the critical scholar's self-awareness and self-monitoring in relation to the "historical specificity" of established disciplinary structures and existing social arrangements.[45] One of the dangers of adopting a global outlook is to assume that there is only one. Classical historians are aware of the difficulties involved in recovering minority or oppositional voices and in reconstructing from them the worldviews, perspectives, and lived experiences of the marginalized. Nevertheless, scholars do not generally reflect on their disciplinary practices, let alone on their social and cultural locations. Phiroze Vasunia has raised this point more than once, connecting the recent surge of interest in ancient multiculturalism with "the historical and ideological concerns of the current generation of scholars" and urging scholars to interrogate their own location and methodological assumptions and ask how and why their particular concerns with ancient multiculturalisms have emerged.[46] These admonitions are of obvious importance to scholars pursuing comparative, transhistorical studies that cut across established boundaries of national or cultural histories. But they also speak to those attempting to craft new global epistemologies that incorporate knowledge sets from two or more disciplines as well as from marginalized, non-Eurocentric systems of knowing.

Scholars in classics will recognize that forms of reflexivity are sewn into the fabric of the discipline. Farrell's provocation to rethink the dichotomy of ancient and modern invokes the language of Plato's Socrates in urging the discipline not to leave such tendentious distinctions unexamined.[47] Studies in the history of classical scholarship dedicated to discussing the discipline's past and future have been a central occupation of the discipline since its foundation in the eighteenth century. Prominent scholars of the nineteenth and twentieth centuries (such as Boeckh, Wilamowitz, Sandys, and Pfeiffer) produced ambitious multivolume histories of classical learning and scholarship. James Porter regrets the displacement of this subfield of classical learning from the center to the periphery of the discipline, lamenting the loss of institutional and pedagogical support for synthetic, holistic methodologies from which the entirety of the field might be surveyed. Despite this nostalgia, Porter confesses that histories of Greek and Roman studies are disconcerting in their contingency, uncomfortable in their dissimilarities, and vertiginous in their changes from generation to generation and from scholar to scholar. "And yet," Porter exclaims,

> one wants to believe that the more reflexivity that gets built into one's discipline, the greater the chances there will be of arriving at . . . what? A truer picture of antiquity? Or of the discipline itself? There is something uncontroversially valid-feeling about knowing how we know what we know.[48]

While the essay does go on to argue for reanimating the history of classical studies, its discomfort with the contingencies of reflexive scholarship and its yearning for "something uncontroversially valid-feeling" reveal the spectrum of possible relations with the materials of the remote past: on one extreme, a sense of nearness and affinity in the perceived continuity of classical learning from antiquity to today, and on the other, a feeling of distance and alienation in the perceived *dis*continuities and the highly fractured and ambiguous historical record. This spectrum of relations mirrors how classical reception studies positions itself as rejecting the diachronic, celebratory macronarratives of the classical tradition in favor of transhistorical relations that emphasize fragmented and discontinuous microhistories.[49]

As we saw in the previous chapter, this spectrum of perspective from nearness to distance also reflects a range of dispositions toward globalizations and global issues, between accounts of globalization as a process that reproduces forms of sameness (nearness, compression, flatness, convergence, homogeneity) and others that see it in terms of processes that foster local expressions of identity (distance, difference, divergence, heterogeneity). The distinction is further illustrated in the contrast between comparative global histories that foreground top-down, sociostructural features of ancient and modern warfare, trade, imperialism, or colonialism (to name just a few) and those that emphasize bottom-up constructions and expressions of local culture in response to transregional cultural and economic flows. Because the former viewpoint has been so widely and influentially disseminated over the past thirty years, a significant balancing effort is required to reorient disciplinary modes of analysis toward the local side of the local-global spectrum. This rebalancing seeks to magnify the diversity of local experiences with globalizing processes and to identity and amplify voices typically omitted from the discourse about globalization in antiquity. But global classics *also* requires engaging with diverse ways of knowing the ancient past and amplifying the voices and perspectives of colleagues outside of Euro-American institutions. Critiques of comparative historical and cultural studies reveal the tendency among comparativists to make transhistorical and transcultural connections without reflecting on their choices of subject, or on the deep histories of scholarship on the issues, and without invoking perspectives of those on one side or the other of the comparison. Vasunia's observation that studies in the comparative imperialisms of Rome and China include few voices of China-based scholars echoes Mittelman's critique of neoliberal accounts of globalization, such as Robert Gilpin's *The Challenge of Global Capitalism*, whose chapters on the Asian financial crisis and migration exclude the views of Asian scholars and the voices of migrants.[50] Over time, these choices normalize the top-down, macro, occidentalist perspectives that view the interests and priorities of the transnational, cosmopolitan elite (global trade, finance, and development agendas) as the drivers of globalization.[51] As we have seen, global studies aims to complement these mainstream, but incomplete narratives with perspectives from across the spectrum of local to global.

But what voices should be represented in the work of the self-monitoring global classicist? Susan George advocates for writing sociologies of the wealthy and powerful on the grounds that scholars who wish to help the poor and powerless should investigate the forces that keep them that way: "Better a sociology of the Pentagon or the Houston country club than of single mothers or L.A. gangs."[52] Mittelman advises the globalization critic to design research and collect data from the diverse standpoints of power. Other scholars of critical global studies draw concepts from a range of critical methodologies to clarify these political and ethical questions involved in the production of knowledge about globalization. Darian-Smith and McCarty view reflexivity as one of the global scholar's most important critical tools for recognizing and incorporating alternative perspectives, subjectivities, and ways of knowing. Their programmatic account of global studies emphasizes the field's contribution to the development of "a global standpoint theory that is deeply intersectional."[53] In other words, global studies draws its critical ethics from feminist standpoint theory, critical race studies and intersectionality, and postcolonial and indigenous studies in recognizing the diverse views and experiences of globalization and global issues: "what makes a methodological strategy global is working across, within, and among plural epistemologies and standpoints to understand a problem or issue from multiple perspectives."[54] As a complement to these critical methodologies, global studies explicitly positions the standpoint of these diverse perspectives within the local-global spectrum. By tracing long-term interactions of local and global, global classics enables scholars to build new analytical frameworks and concepts, to make otherwise unseen, transhistorical connections, and to foster new levels of ethicopolitical solidarity with the potential to address global forms of injustice and inequality.

Reflexive approaches to the study of globalization and global issues are therefore closely related to transformative practices aimed at challenging narratives that view established structures of power and social relations as the natural, even inevitable outcomes of history. For Mark Neufeld, critical reflexivity means interrogating the assumption of the world as given (including institutions, relations, and arrangements of power) by investigating their origins and history and by illuminating alternatives to the existing order:

> what is required is a way of thinking about globalisation (i) that is multidimensional, paying due attention to the qualitative dimensions of

themes including (but not limited to) the state, democracy, culture, and world order; (ii) embodies a critical, solidaristic ethics which can serve as the basis for collective action; and (iii) offers an analytic framework which directs our attention to the contradictory nature of the processes of globalisation, and the opportunities for emancipatory practice afforded by the resulting instabilities in the established order.[55]

The critical ethics that Neufeld imagines here uses multilevel, transhistorical thinking about global issues to seek out opportunities for challenging established structures and paradigms. These opportunities emerge from several sources: the refusal to reduce globalization to simply processes of political, economic, and cultural change; the identification of shared experiences of inequality and injustice, which can foster the growth of solidaric consciousness; and the recognition of contradictions within the crises and unsustainable processes of globalization, which may serve as bases for challenging the status quo. These contradictions are defined as oppositional relations that are at the same time necessary for and destructive to the processes and forces of globalization. These relations are evident, for instance, in the opposition of homogeneity and heterogeneity in globalization narratives, in which the potential for the oppression and erasure of difference in fact has the opposite effect of *producing* new forms and expressions of difference. Like the authors in the collection by Appelbaum and Robinson, Neufeld emphasizes critical approaches to globalization that clarify its role in the planetwide reproduction of social inequalities. By embracing a critical ethics that seeks to identify shared experiences of oppression, global studies remains open to (and even welcomes) forms of social criticism that challenge the asymmetries of power and seek to bring about a more just global society.

Building on this critical global ethics, the new field of global classics has a strong interest in applying its knowledge of the dynamics shaping globalizations in and since antiquity. Scholars of global classics seek to challenge the established structures and paradigms within classical studies and make transhistorical connections that reflect diverse standpoints across the spectrum of local to global. The field incorporates theories from across disciplines to facilitate the holistic study of multidimensional global issues through time from diverse perspectives. Global approaches entail not only questioning the predominant spatiotemporal boundaries that inscribe and apportion classics but also adopting an issue-based approach to research. War, inequality, migration, xenophobia, and terrorism are all major geopolitical issues shaped by the contexts in which they occur; many features of the modern, global arrangement of power, peoples, and resources have come into existence through globalizing processes that have unfolded unevenly across boundaries and over centuries. But to look backward in history to perceived origins or comparable issues perpetuates an illusion that knowledge can simply be extracted from ancient sources and transferred into modern contexts. On the contrary, comparisons of this sort require careful contextual analysis free from the illusion that ancient contexts may be easily mapped onto modern ones. The path is fraught with perils ranging from the oversimplification (at best) to the complete distortion (at worst) of complex problems, in either case leading to flawed readings, theories, recommendations, and policies. It is in this process of discernment that global classics researchers and educators take active roles.

Far from occupying a remote corner of the humanities, classicists, archaeologists, and ancient historians are advantageously positioned to engage on a variety of global issues, especially (but not only) when knowledge of antiquity is put explicitly into play. Public responses to global issues through classics take many forms along both traditional and nontraditional avenues. Scholars aiming to promote disciplinary change to a wide audience within the field have published reflexive histories and appraisals of classical scholarship in established journals. The editorials by Patrice Rankine and Mira Seo in volume 140 (2019) of the *American Journal of Philology* implicate classics in forms of cultural erasure and marginalization, while challenging scholars with ways to do better.[56] Another form of public, global classics involves entering into public debates in which ancient sources are invoked in support of reactionary agendas. Forms of self-publishing, such as blogs and podcasts, by virtue of being free, widely accessible, and infinitely sharable can reach a wider public than even top-tier academic journals (and especially those locked behind paywalls). Public classics projects such as *PHAROS*, a collaborative platform hosted and curated by Curtis Dozier at Vassar College, can not only disseminate responses to the appropriations of antiquity by hate groups but may also help to control the spread of hate through the virtual ecosystem by ensuring that those searching the global internet for information about antiquity find alternatives to racist, misogynistic, and other reactionary views. In the three years since its inception in the fall of 2017, *PHAROS* has published nearly 100 essays, editorials, and responses to such appropriations of Greco-Roman culture, often exposing their errors, omissions, and inaccuracies.[57] Not all such appropriations of antiquity are as violent and hateful as those documented by *PHAROS*. Subtler appropriations exist, such as the concept of the "Thucydides Trap", which sees violent conflict as inevitable whenever a rising power threatens to displace a ruling one.[58] Johanna Hanink's 2019 translation of selected speeches and debates from Thucydides for Princeton's series, *Ancient Wisdom for Modern Readers*, responds to readings of Thucydides popularized in neoconservative media and policy circles.[59] Subtitled *An Ancient*

Guide to Foreign Policy," Hanink's project is also a guide to the current, Thucydidean moment that acknowledges how Athens (at the same time as it produced the wise deliberations and exhortations about war that Thucydides documents in his speeches) pursued disastrous policies, leading ultimately to its own self-destruction.

These examples of public forms of classical scholarship reveal the potential of critical, transdisciplinary research to advance knowledge and awareness of transhistorical, global issues. My view is not that all scholars should operate in these modes all of the time, but that something vital is lost if at least some scholars are not pursuing transdisciplinary research and contributing to public debates some of the time. In considering the future prospects of classical reception studies, James Porter makes an impassioned appeal for classicists to enter and contribute to public debates:

> the engaged public intellectual who not only can create new public audiences for the field and the academy at large, but who also can enter into debates within the larger public sphere and can contribute in ways that only a perspective on the very origins of western culture and political life can afford.[60]

Porter's exhortation is in line with his view of classics as foundational to the discourse of modernity and, therefore, uniquely positioned to challenge and subvert modernizing ideologies. From this perspective, the contribution of classical scholars to public debates can be attributed to the field's claim to knowledge of the origins of modern culture and political life. While there is surely much to be gained from exploring the place of classics in these narratives of origins, such teleologies are themselves among modernity's most problematic byproducts. The notion that the public role of classics is circumscribed by the field's perspectives on "Western" culture and values is highly limiting, dependent on undertheorized period logics that are not politically neutral.

By contrast, globalizing classics implies the recognition of alternative antiquities and the amplification of voices from outside of the field's traditional spatial and temporal boundaries—and, importantly, from outside of the field's traditional centers of knowledge production. By combining a transdisciplinary, problem-based approach to globalization with a holistic, deep historical perspective, global classics offers a powerful analytical toolkit for studying issues impacting the lives of billions of people around the globe. These tools are not limited either to the study of the ancient "West" or to the teleological, historicist orientation of modernity, but rather they are open to the connections and disruptions of globalization across spatiotemporal borders. A globalized perspective reminds scholars that just as

98 *Transdisciplinary*

the minority populations of Europe and North America are the majority of the global population, so too most humans of the ancient past inhabited lifeways outside of the elite, urbanized centers that are the focus of so much historical research. Their voices and perspectives are underrepresented by our sources in the same way that today's global majorities remain underrepresented in the world's major universities. They are nevertheless disproportionately vulnerable to the negative impacts of globalization, such as war, migration, inequality, and climate change. The public commitment of global classics scholars therefore is not limited to excavating the historical origins of the so-called "West", but rather involves recovering the fullest diversity of perception and experience of globalization through time by identifying the field's blind spots and denials of coevalness and by confronting its history of exclusion and marginalization. Critical reflexivity fosters transformative practice through the formation of transhistorical politicoethical solidarity that can serve as a basis for collective action. Global processes are at work every day in the lives of billions of humans. Those who aim to study and impact these processes need ways to transcend traditional disciplinary boundaries and ways to engage with colleagues, students, and neighbors across our universities, in our communities, and around the world.

Conclusion

This chapter has sought to promote transdisciplinarity, the deliberate crossing and blending of theories, methods, and perspectives, as essential to the investigation of globalization and global issues. Researchers operating in transhistorical comparativist modes cannot draw confidence in applying the conceptual categories of global inquiry (i.e., mobility, inequality, imperialism) to ancient worlds from *intra*disciplinary engagement alone. The mixing of analytical methods and interpretive frames is essential in addressing questions of long-term global change, because complex global issues are rarely fixed or static but unfold unevenly and are experienced by people in divergent ways. Global studies scholars embrace transdisciplinary research methods because globalizing processes encompass both ends of the local-global spectrum, requiring researchers to combine knowledge sets, and because complex global issues have more than one side.[61] Reflection on the plurality of experiences and perceptions of global issues through time means acknowledging the limitations of one's own time and place and assumptions about the world. This critical reflexivity is perhaps the global classicist's most essential tool, facilitating the development of a transhistorical, solidaristic ethic that connects with perspectives and experiences that are absent from top-down, macrohistorical narratives about globalization. By uncovering the origins and histories of our assumptions about globalization, we can refocus attention on the role that classics has played in promoting certain narratives, while excluding others, and facilitate the recovery of alternative voices, epistemologies, and standpoints. The deterritorializing and antiperiodizing approach of global classics is meant to free researchers from the intellectual confines of methodological nationalism and from the teleology of modernity, while helping them pursue research questions and projects that are distinctly global and inclusive.

Conceived in this way, the pursuit of global research in classics also enables and contributes to the pursuit of social justice objectives. The pursuit of global research demands a transdisciplinary approach that is sensitive to the many possible manifestations of global issues across space (local, regional, national, transnational), time (periodic, diachronic, transhistorical, *événementielle*, social history, *longue durée*, deep history, big history), and social category (culture, economy, politics; but also race, ethnicity, class, gender, religion, age, and ability). These dimensions intersect in the lived experience of globalization, and they generate distinct perspectives on global issues. Researchers crafting questions and designing approaches to global issues in the present day alone can be overwhelmed by all of these transecting elements. When one factors in the deep historical dimensions of global classics, the possibilities may seem infinite. Fortunately, while global research requires sensitivity to these intersecting levels and dimensions, researchers do not need to investigate every manifestation of an issue from every perspective: they should rather recognize that global issues operate across dimensions and intersect at various levels and be prepared to acknowledge that these intersections may be among their most interesting and important features. Scholars may cultivate this awareness by framing problem-based research questions around specific global issues (such as conflict, migration, inequality, imperialism, and others) and by drawing on the growing literature on those issues. While much research is still being generated by scholars working within traditional disciplines in the humanities and social sciences, an increasing variety of relevant scholarship is emerging from within critical, transdisciplinary fields. This book has argued that familiarity with the diverse literature on global issues and active transdisciplinary engagement between classics and global studies can facilitate the formulation of relevant research questions, leading to new global forms of knowledge about ancient worlds and their receptions through time.

Notes

1 Nederveen Pieterse 2013: 511.
2 Steger 2017: 86.
3 Steger and Wahlrab 2017: 87.
4 Nederveen Pieterse 2013: 505–506.
5 Steger and Wahlrab 2017: 109; drawing in turn from Klein 2017: 29–30.

6 Darian-Smith and McCarty 2017: chapter 3.
7 Collingwood and Wright 1965: 641, no. 2092. https://romaninscriptionsofbritain. org/inscriptions/2092 accessed September 26, 2020.
8 Stoll 2007: 453. The association of *disciplina* and its virtues with margins should be investigated; Socrates' hardiness and self-mastery were also most famously on display while he was on campaign in Potidea, far from Athens (cf. Plato *Symposium* 219e-220d).
9 Foucault 1975: 162.
10 *Ibid.* 258.
11 Gieryn 1983: 791–792.
12 Steger and Wahlrab 2017: 86–87 and bibliography.
13 Klein 2017: 16; Choi and Pak 2006: 359 and *passim*; Alvarogonzález 2011: 387–389; Steger and Wahlrab 2017: 90–94.
14 Alvarogonzález 2011: 394; Choi and Pak 2006.
15 Klein 2017.
16 Steger and Wahlrab 2017: 94–95, with references to Tomlinson 1999.
17 Steger and Wahlrab 2017: 96–108.
18 Beard and Henderson 1995: 63, emphasis in the original.
19 Segal 1995: 2.
20 Farrell 2019: 214.
21 *Ibid.* 215 with emphasis added.
22 Hayot 2011: 741.
23 Not, however, uniquely contrasting as a comparison with, for example, Medieval Studies and Renaissance Studies reveals, though Farrell (2019: 215) notes that these subjects are often represented by lesser-status entities such as programs, than by departments.
24 Blumenberg 1983; Davis 2008; McClure 2015; see discussion in Chapter 2.
25 Bakhtin 1981: 84.
26 *Ibid.* 90.
27 For example, Spawforth 2018.
28 Hayot 2011: 745.
29 Segal 1995: 9.
30 Cf. Steger's (2017: 13) pithy definition of globalization, which operates "across world-time and world-space."
31 Klein 2017: 30.
32 Segal 1995: 8.
33 Appadurai 1990: 295; Hodos 2017a: 7–8.
34 Steger and Wahlrab 2017: 154.
35 Bourdieu 2003: 18.
36 *Ibid.* 23–24 with emphasis in the original.
37 Robinson 2005: 13.
38 Appelbaum and Robinson 2005: xiii.
39 George 2005: 3, 6.
40 Robinson 2005: 15.
41 Mittelman 2005: 20–21.
42 *Ibid.* 24; cf. Darian-Smith 2015.
43 Mittelman 2005: 25.
44 Whitmarsh 2010; Vlassopoulos 2013; Witcher 2017: 645–648.
45 Robinson 2005: 11.
46 Vasunia 2005: 180, 2011: 225.

47 Farrell 2019: 217.
48 Porter 2008: 470–471.
49 Güthenke 2009; see discussion in Chapter 2.
50 E.g. Mittelman 2005: 23–24; Vasunia 2011; cf. Darian-Smith and McCarty 2017: 37–39, 126–127, 152–177.
51 Sklair 2005: 59–61.
52 George 2005: 8.
53 Darian-Smith and McCarty 2017: 175, 226.
54 *Ibid*. 175. For standpoint theory, see Smith 1977; for intersectionality, see Collins and Bilge 2016.
55 Neufeld 2001: 97; cf 1995: ch.3.
56 Rankine 2019; Seo 2019.
57 http://pages.vassar.edu/pharos/ accessed 10/20/20. Likewise, between 2015 and 2020, the online journal *EIDOLON* (https://eidolon.pub/) published essays confronting the discipline's colonialist, heteronormative, and racist history.
58 E.g. Allison 2017; discussion in Bloxham 2018: 193–203 and 231.
59 Hanink 2019.
60 Porter 2008: 479.
61 Darian-Smith and McCarty 2017: 148–151.

Epilogue

The globalization of classics is already underway, but it is an unfinished project, barely begun in fact. Many connections remain to be made among the forms of research discussed in this book and among the work of other scholars and activists whose contributions to knowledge of global issues have fallen outside of the book's scope. Nevertheless, I have attempted to synthesize a vibrant decades-long development in classics, as parts of the field have come to embrace concepts and theories of globalization, molding them to various purposes and viewing ancient sources and materials through a global lens.

Many intellectual temptations and pitfalls obstruct the panoramas of transhistorical interconnectivities and cultural flows that are the object of the global study of antiquities. Interdisciplinary, multilevel, and transhistorical thinking is challenging and unfamiliar, especially in a discipline whose borders have been so heavily patrolled as those of classics.[1] Because classical studies historically privileges perspectives from particular strata of knowledge, multilevel and multicentric methodologies offer a contrasting and perhaps disorienting view. Global approaches to classics are prone to many of the same problems of scope, reductionism, aggregation, and generalization as global studies and other comparative methodologies. Comparisons across long expanses of space and time require large, meta concepts, which can tempt scholars to privilege structures and macro perspectives over individuals and agency/subjectivity (as in the critique of world-systems that it ignores the roles of local class struggles). The reliance of global studies (and hence, to a degree, of global classics) on large-scale, meta concepts and macronarratives may be suspicious to scholars of antiquity, trained by postmodernism to look for diversity and fragmentation.[2] A list of fallacies and cognitive challenges to the new field would include:[3]

- *The problem of scale and generalization*, as in the assumption that what appears valid at one level of analysis remains valid at other levels.

Epilogue   103

This is also an empirical challenge, as the field must find innovative ways to generate new knowledge out of data collected from a variety of multilevel perspectives.
- *The problem of cultural aggregation*, adopting language that elides differences within identity communities and lumps together, for example, Greeks, Romans, Etruscans, and Phoenicians. These terms, which are common (and perhaps sometimes valid) at a superficial level of discourse, lose their integrity in the context of interactions at smaller scales. How can we tell from the available evidence when or whether a particular cultural identity group comes into being through different processes?
- *The problem of essentialism and homogenization*, which can mean homogenization of processes (e.g., conflict, migration, enslavement, colonialism), categories of evidence (e.g., material culture, texts), or identity communities (e.g., ethnicity, class, age, gender, race, ability). Like identities, processes and interactions themselves are not fixed and unchanging concepts, but contextual and culturally informed. What is needed is a "systematic mapping and super-positioning of typologies."[4]
- *The problems of the ethics and politics of representation*. Recovery of marginalized or minority voices from cultural traditions dominated by elite perspectives is a difficult task—impossible, some have argued.
- *The problem of the top-down view* of history and globalization by cultural elites (ancient and modern). From the 30,000-mile view, it is relatively easy to imagine away the borders on a map and to conceptualize large-scale social and economic networks and macro processes, but it is much harder to identify and describe the shifting roles of individual links in the great chains of globalization and tradition.
- *The problem of scope*. The common perception that global means everything among academics outside of the field may create the impression that the field lacks focus. This challenge faces interdisciplinary programs, like global studies, whose multilevel, multicentric approaches can appear "to revel in the mesmerizing complexity of it all."[5] The field must develop ways to collect, organize, and compare relevant case studies from diverse methodologies and ways to produce and disseminate new knowledge. As this challenge involves significant institution building (professional associations, journals, conferences, programs, etc.), it will take a generational effort to meet.

Above all, these problems reveal the need for global classics to be a *critical* global classics: aware of the different kinds of useful knowledge about globalization and antiquity and how these diverse knowledge sets overlap, and willing to put this knowledge to work in public critique of social impacts and dynamics of globalization. Because interest in globalization reflects contemporary priorities and ideological concerns, scholars of antiquity should especially consider their own cultural assumptions and social location. That involves asking why these questions about globalizing classics have emerged now, why they have emerged in these particular ways, and how our own assumptions about and experiences of globalization impact our study of globalizing processes through history.

In marshaling the three powerful modalities that structure this book (transborder, transhistorical, and transdisciplinary), scholars of global classics advance a complex agenda, perhaps best understood in reference to a fourth trans- concept, the *transgressive*. This term denotes the decentering efforts and the blurring of borders and boundaries, as well as the vital connection between the production of knowledge and the pursuit of societal transformation. The history of interdisciplinarity and transdisciplinarity tracks with movements that not only critique disciplinarity but link that critique to questions of sociopolitical justice.[6] The problem-oriented, socially engaged approach of global studies reflects this trend. The field nourishes those imaginative faculties that help us address global problems of social well-being and their influence in our daily lives: "It allows people to consider migration, resist state violence, seek social redress, and design new forms of civic association and collaboration, often across national boundaries."[7] The transdisciplinary methodology of global classics, synthesizing literary and historiographical interpretation with the study of material cultures, offers a model for holistic approaches to the complex issues of transhistorical human interconnectedness. In order to meet these pressing demands, global classics must address these challenges and establish new and useful standards of knowledge if it is to deliver successfully on its potential and become a major new field and approach.

Notes

1 duBois 2010: 25 and n.50.
2 Hodos 2010a: 5–9, 2010b: 81–83.
3 This list is modeled on Nederveen Pieterse 2013: 510.
4 Rowlands 2010: 237.
5 McCarty 2014: 284; Steger and Wahlrab 2017: 16.
6 Vickers 1997; Klein 2017: 30.
7 Appadurai 2000: 6.

Works cited

Abu-Lughod, J. L. 1989. *Beyond European Hegemony: The World System A.D. 1250–1350*. Oxford: Oxford University Press.
Abu-Lughod, J. L. 1993. "Discontinuities and Persistence: One World System or a Succession of Systems?" Pp. 278–291 in A. G. Frank and B. K. Gills eds., *The World System: Five Hundred Years or Five Thousand?* Abingdon, UK: Routledge.
Adler, E. 2016. *Classics, the Culture Wars, and Beyond*. Ann Arbor: University of Michigan Press.
Albert, M. 1999. "Complex Governance and Morality in World Society." *Global Society* 13 (1): 77–93.
Allison, G. 2017. *Destined for War: Can America and China Escape Thucydides's Trap?* New York: Mariner Books.
Alonso-Núñez, J. M. 1990. "The Emergence of Universal Historiography from the 4th to the 2nd Centuries B.C." Pp. 173–192 in H. Verdin, G. Schepens, and E. de Keyser eds., *Purposes of History: Studies in Greek Historiography from the 4th to the 2nd Centuries B.C.* Leuven: Dack and Dessel.
Alonso-Núñez, J. M. 2004. "Globalizzazione ed imperialismo romano." *Patavium* 23: 3–12.
Alvarogonzález, D. 2011. "Multidisciplinarity, Interdisciplinarity, Transdisciplinarity, and the Sciences." *International Studies in the Philosophy of Science* 25 (4): 387–403. doi: 10.1080/02698595.2011.623366
Amin, S. 1989. *Eurocentrism*. New York: Monthly Review Press.
Amin, S. 1993. "The Ancient World-System versus the Modern Capitalist World-System." Pp. 247–277 in A. G. Frank and B. K. Gills eds., *The World System: Five Hundred Years or Five Thousand?* Abingdon, UK: Routledge.
Antonaccio, C. 1995. "Lefkandi and Homer." Pp. 5–28 in Ø. Andersen and M. Dickie eds., *Homer's World: Fiction, Tradition, Reality*. Bergen: P. Aströms Förlag.
Appadurai, A. 1990. "Disjuncture and Difference in the Global Cultural Economy." *Theory, Culture & Society* 7: 291–310.
Appadurai, A. 2000. "Grassroots Globalization and the Research Imagination." *Public Culture* 12 (1): 1–19.
Appelbaum, R. P. and W. I. Robinson. 2005. "Introduction: Toward a Critical Globalization Studies: Continued Debates, New Directions, Neglected Topics." Pp. xi–xxxiii in R. P. Appelbaum and W. I. Robinson eds., *Critical Globalization Studies*. New York: Routledge.

Works cited

Arendt, H. 1958. *The Human Condition*. Chicago: University of Chicago Press.
Austin, M. 2006. *The Hellenistic World from Alexander to the Roman Conquest: A Selection of Ancient Sources in Translation*. Second edition. Cambridge: Cambridge University Press.
Bacigalupo, M. 2007. "Tradition in 1919: Pound, Eliot and the 'Historical Method'." Pp. 103–116 in G. Cianci and J. Harding eds., *T. S. Eliot and the Concept of Tradition*. Cambridge: Cambridge University Press.
Bagnall, R. S. 1995. *Reading Papyri, Writing Ancient History*. Abingdon, UK: Routledge.
Bagnall, R. S. and R. Cribiore. 2006. *Women's Letters from Ancient Egypt*. Ann Arbor: University of Michigan.
Bailey, C. ed. 1924. *The Legacy of Rome*. Oxford: Oxford University Press.
Bakhtin, M. 1981. "Forms of Time and of the Chronotope in the Novel." In *The Dialogic Imagination*. Austin: University Texas Press.
Barber, B. R. 1992. "Jihad vs. McWorld." *The Atlantic* 269 (3): unpaginated.
Baron, C. A. 2013. *Timaeus of Tauromenium and Hellenistic Historiography*. Cambridge: Cambridge University Press.
Barth, F. 1969. *Ethnic Groups and Boundaries: The Social Organization of Cultural Difference*. Boston: Little, Brown and Company.
Basch, L., N. Glick Schiller, and C. Szanton-Blanc. 1994. *Nations Unbound: Transnational Projects, Postcolonial Predicaments, and Deterritorialized Nation-States*. Langhorne, PA: Gordon & Breach.
Beard, M. and J. Henderson. 1995. *Classics: A Very Short Introduction*. Oxford: Oxford University Press.
Beecroft, A. 2010. *Authorship and Cultural Identity in Early Greece and China: Patterns of Literary Circulation*. Cambridge: Cambridge University Press.
Beecroft, A. 2015. *An Ecology of World Literature: From Antiquity to the Present Day*. London: Verso.
Benjamin, C. 2014. "'But from This Time Forth History Becomes a Connected Whole': State Expansion and the Origins of Universal History." *Journal of Global History* 9: 357–378.
ben-Jochannan, Y. A. A. 1988. *Africa: Mother of Western Civilization*. Baltimore: Black Classic Press.
Bentley, J. 2004. "Globalizing History and Historicizing Globalization." *Globalizations* 1 (1): 69–81.
Berghoff, W. 1967. *Palladius De Gentibus Indiae et Bragmanibus*. Meisenheim am Glan: Verlag Anton Hain.
Bernal, M. 1987. *Black Athena: The Afroasiatic Roots of Classical Civilization*. New Brunswick: Rutgers University Press.
Bernard, P. 1969. "Quatrième campagne de fouilles à Aï Khanoum (Bactriane)." *Comptes Rendus de l'Académie des inscriptions et belles-lettres*: 313–355.
Bernard, P. 1970. "Campagne de fouilles 1969 à Aï Khanoum en Afghanistan." *Comptes Rendus de l'Académie des inscriptions et belles-lettres*: 301–349.
Bernard, P. 1976. "Campagne de fouilles 1975 à Aï Khanoum (Afghanistan)." *Comptes rendus de l'Académie des Inscriptions et Belles-Lettres*: 287–322.

Bernard, P. 1978. "Campagne de fouilles 1976-1977 à Aï Khanoum (Afghanistan)." *Comptes rendus de l'Académie des Inscriptions et Belles-Lettres*: 421–463.
Bernard, P. 1980. "Campagne de fouilles 1978 à Aï Khanoum (Afghanistan)." *Comptes rendus de l'Académie des Inscriptions et Belles-Lettres*: 435–459.
Bintliff, J. 1997. "Regional Survey, Demography, and the Rise of Complex Societies in the Ancient Aegean: Core- Periphery, Neo-Malthusian, and Other Interpretive Models." *JFA* 24: 1–38.
Birot, P. 1964. *La Méditerrannnée et le moyen Orient*. Second edition. Paris: Presses universitaires de France.
Blackbourn, D. 2012. "'The Horologe of Time': Periodization in History." *Proceedings of the Modern Language Association* 127 (2): 301–307.
Bloxham, J. A. 2018. *Ancient Greece and American Conservatism: Classical Influences on the Modern Right*. London: I. B. Tauris.
Blumenberg, H. 1983. *The Legitimacy of the Modern Age*. Second edition. Boston, MA: M.I.T. Press.
Bolgar, R. R. ed. 1971. *Classical Influences on European Culture A.D. 500–1500*. Cambridge: Cambridge University Press.
Bolgar, R. R. 1973 [1954]. *The Classical Heritage and Its Beneficiaries*. Cambridge: Cambridge University Press.
Boroditsky, L. 2000. "Metaphoric Structuring: Understanding Time through Spatial Metaphors." *Cognition* 75: 1–28.
Bosher, K. ed. 2012. *Theater Outside Athens: Drama in Greek Sicily and South Italy*. Cambridge: Cambridge University Press.
Bostick, D. 2020. "Not for All: Nostalgic Distortions as a Weapon of Segregation in Secondary Classics." *American Journal of Philology* 141 (2): 283–306.
Bourdieu, P. 2003. *Firing Back: Against the Tyranny of the Market 2*. New York: New Press.
Bradley, R. 1991. "Ritual, Time, and History." *World Archaeology* 23: 209–219.
Braudel, F. 1980. *On History*. Translated by Sarah Matthews. Chicago: University of Chicago Press.
Brunt, P. A. 1976. *Arrian: Anabasis of Alexander. Volume I Books 1–4*. Cambridge, MA: Harvard University Press.
Budelmann, F. and J. Haubold. 2008. "Reception and Tradition." Pp. 13–25 in L. Hardwick and C. Stray eds., *A Companion to Classical Receptions*. Malden, MA: Wiley-Blackwell.
Burian, P. 2011. "Athenian Tragedy as Democratic Discourse." Pp. 95–118 in D. M. Carter ed., *Why Athens? A Reappraisal of Tragic Politics*. Oxford: Oxford University Press.
Burn, A. R. 1936. *The World of Hesiod: A Study of the Greek Middle Ages, c. 900–700 B.C.* New York: E. P. Dutton and Co.
Butler, S. 2016. "Introduction: On the Origin of 'Deep Classics'." Pp. 1–18 in S. Butler ed., *Deep Classics: Rethinking Classical Reception*. London: Bloomsbury.
Cairncross, F. 1997. *The Death of Distance: How the Communication Revolution Will Change Our Lives*. Cambridge, MA: Harvard Business School.
Canali De Rossi, Filippo. 2004. *Iscrizioni dello Estremo Oriente greco: Un repertorio. Inschriften griechischer Städte aus Kleinasien*. volume 65. Bonn: Dr. Rudolf Habelt.

108 Works cited

Carter, D. M. 2007. *The Politics of Greek Tragedy*. Bristol: Phoenix Press.
Casanova, P. 2004. *The World Republic of Letters*. Translated by M. B. DeBevoise. Cambridge, MA: Harvard University Press.
Casanova, P. 2005. "Literature as a World." *New Left Review* 31: 71–90.
Casasanto, D. and L. Boroditsky. 2008. "Time in the Mind: Using Space to Think about Time." *Cognition* 106: 579–593.
Castells, M. 1996. *The Rise of the Network Society*. Oxford: Blackwell Publishers.
Chakrabarty, D. 2000. *Provincializing Europe: Postcolonial Thought and Historical Difference*. Princeton: Princeton University Press.
Chakrabarty, D. 2002. *Habitations of Modernity: Essays in the Wake of Subaltern Studies*. Chicago: University of Chicago Press.
Chase-Dunn, C. and T. D. Hall. 1997. *Rise and Demise: Comparing World-Systems*. Westview Press.
Cheah, P. 2016. *What Is a World?: On Postcolonial Literature as World Literature*. Durham, NC: Duke University Press.
Cherry, J. F. 2004. "Mediterranean Island Prehistory: What's Different and What's New." Pp. 233–248 in S. M. Fitzpatrick ed., *Voyages of Discovery: The Archaeology of Islands*. Westport, CT: Praeger.
Choi, B. C. K. and A. W. P. Pak. 2006. "Multidisciplinarity, Interdisciplinarity and Transdisciplinarity in Health Research, Services, Education, and Policy: 1. Definitions, Objectives, and Evidence of Effectiveness." *Clinical and Investigative Medicine* 29: 351–364.
Christian, D. 2005. *Maps of Time: An Introduction to Big History*. Berkeley and Los Angeles: University of California Press.
Clarke, K. 1999. *Between Geography and History: Hellenistic Constructions of the Roman World*. Oxford: Oxford University Press.
Coldstream, J. N. 2003 [1977]. *Geometric Greece*. Second edition. Abingdon, UK: Routledge.
Cole, A. and D. Vance Smith. 2010. *The Legitimacy of the Middle Ages: On the Unwritten History of Theory*. Durham, NC: Duke University Press.
Collingwood, R. G. and R. P. Wright. 1965. *The Roman Inscriptions of Britain, Vol. 1: Inscriptions on Stone*. Oxford: Oxford University Press..
Collins, P. H. and S. Bilge. 2016. *Intersectionality*. Cambridge: Polity.
Connor, W. R. 1989. "City Dionysia and Athenian Democracy." *Classica et mediaevalia* 40: 7–32.
Cunliffe, B. 1988. *Greeks, Romans and Barbarians: Spheres of Interaction*. London: Batsford.
Damrosch, D. 2003. *What Is World Literature?* Princeton: Princeton University Press.
Danforth, L. M. 1984. "The Ideological Context of the Search for Continuities in Greek Culture." *Journal of Modern Greek Studies* 2: 53–85.
Darian-Smith, E. 2015. "Global Studies: The Handmaiden of Neoliberalism." *Globalizations* 12 (2): 164–168.
Darian-Smith, E. and P. McCarty. 2017. *The Global Turn: Theories, Research Designs, and Methods for Global Studies*. Berkeley: University of California Press.
Davies, J. K. 2002. "Greek History: A Discipline in Transformation." Pp. 225–246 in T. P. Wiseman ed., *Classics in Progress: Essays on Ancient Greece and Rome*. Oxford: Oxford University Press.

Works cited

Davis, K. 2008. *Periodization and Sovereignty, How Ideas of Feudalism & Secularization Govern the Politics of Time.* Philadelphia: University of Pennsylvania Press.
Davis, K. and N. Altschul. 2009. *Medievalisms in the Postcolonial World: The Idea of "the Middle Ages" Outside Europe.* Baltimore: Johns Hopkins University Press.
della Porta, D. et al. 2006. *Globalization from below: Transnational Activists and Protest Networks.* Minneapolis, MN: University of Minnesota.
Denecke, W. 2014. *Classical World Literatures. Sino-Japanese and Greco-Roman Comparisons.* Oxford: Oxford University Press.
Di Castro, A. A. 2005. "The Barbarisation of Bactria." In *Cultural Interaction in Afghanistan, c. 300 BCE to 300 CE.* Working Paper 5, Centre of South Asian Studies. Clayton: Monash University Press.
Diop, C. A. 1955. *Nations nègres et culture.* Paris: Présence Africaine.
Diop, C. A. 1967. *Antériorité des civilizations nègres: mythe ou vérité historique.* Paris: Présence Africaine.
Diop, C. A. 1981. *Civilisation ou barbarie: anthropologie sans complaisance.* Paris: Présence Africaine.
Dirlik, A. 2007. *Global Modernity: Modernity in the Age of Global Capitalism.* Boulder: Paradigm Publishers.
Dominik, W. J. 2007. "Africa." Pp. 117-131 in C. W. Kallendorf ed., *A Companion to the Classical Tradition.* Malden, MA: Wiley-Blackwell.
Doniger, W. 1999. *Splitting the Difference: Gender and Myth in Ancient Greece and India.* Chicago: University of Chicago Press.
Dougherty, C. and L. Kurke. 2003. *The Cultures within Ancient Greek Culture: Contact, Conflict, Collaboration.* Cambridge: Cambridge University Press.
Drews, R. 1963. "Ephoros and History Written κατὰ γένος." *American Journal of Philology* 84: 244–255.
DuBois, P. 2001. *Trojan Horses: Saving the Classics from Conservatives.* New York: New York University.
DuBois, P. 2010. *Out of Athens: The New Ancient Greeks.* Cambridge, MA: Harvard University Press.
Duncan, A. 2011. "Nothing to Do with Athens? Tragedians at the Courts of Tyrants." Pp. 69–84 in D. M. Carter ed., *Why Athens? A Reappraisal of Tragic Politics.* Oxford: Oxford University Press..
Dunne, T. 1999. "The Spectre of Globalization." *Indiana Journal of Global Legal Studies* 7 (1): 17–33.
Eisenstadt, S. N. 2000. "Multiple Modernities." *Daedalus* 129 (1): 1–29.
Ekholm, K. and J. Friedman. 1993. "'Capital' Imperialism and Exploitation in Ancient World Systems." Pp. 59–80 in A. G. Frank and B. K. Gills eds., *The World System: Five Hundred Years or Five Thousand?* Abingdon, UK: Routledge.
Eliot, T. S. 1932. *Selected Essays.* London: Faber and Faber.
Ellis, J. R. 1981. "Macedonia under Philip." Pp. 146–165 in M. B. Hatzopoulos and L. D. Loukopoulos eds., *Philip of Macedon.* London: Heinemann.
Eriksen, T. H. 2007. *Globalization.* New York: Berg.
Fabian, J. 2014. *Time and the Other: How Anthropology Makes Its Object.* New York: Columbia University Press.
Farrell, J. 2019. "Ancient and Modern: A Critical Reflection." *TAPA* 149 (2): 211–218.

Works cited

Ferguson, M. 1992. "The Mythology about Globalization." *European Journal of Communication* 7: 69–93.
Finley, M. I. 1982 [1954]. *The World of Odysseus*. New York: Review of Books.
Flynn, D. O. and A. Giráldez. 2006. "Globalization Began in 1571." Pp. 208–222 in B. K. Gills and W. R. Thompson eds., *Globalization and Global History*. Abingdon, UK: Routledge.
Fontanella, F., ed. and trans. 2007. *A Roma: Elio Aristide*. Pisa: Scuola Normale Superiore.
Foucault, M. 1975. *Surveiller et punir: Naissance de la prison*. Paris: Gallimard.
Frank, A. G. and B. K. Gills. 1993. "The 5,000-Year World System: An Interdisciplinary Introduction." Pp. 3–55 in A. G. Frank and B. K. Gills eds., *The World System: Five Hundred Years or Five Thousand?* Abingdon, UK: Routledge.
Fulbrook, M. 2002. *Historical Theory*. Abingdon, UK: Routledge.
Fusco, S.-A. 2003. "Il Tardoantico, la 'globalizzazione' e le crisi della giustizia." *Studia et documenta historíae et iuris* 69: 413–426.
Fynn-Paul, J. 2009. "Empire, Monotheism and Slavery in the Greater Mediterranean Region from Antiquity to the Early Modern Era." *Past & Present* 205: 3–40.
Gabriel, R. A. 2010. *Philip II of Macedonia: Greater Than Alexander*. Washington, DC: Potomac Books Inc.
George, S. 2005. "If You Want to Be Relevant: Advice to the Academic from a Scholar-Activist." Pp. 3–9 in R. P. Appelbaum and W. I. Robinson eds., *Critical Globalization Studies*. New York: Routledge.
Giddens, A. 1990. *The Consequences of Modernity*. Cambridge: Polity Press.
Gieryn, T. F. 1983. "Boundary-Work and the Demarcation of Science from Non-Science: Strains and Interests in Professional Ideologies of Scientists." *American Sociological Review* 48: 781–795.
Gills, B. K. 2004. "The Turning of the Tide." *Globalizations* 1 (1): 1–6.
Gills, B. K. and W. R. Thompson. 2006. "Globalizations, Global Histories and Historical Hlobalities." Pp. 1–15 in B. K. Gills and W. R. Thompson eds., *Globalization and Global History*. Abingdon, UK: Routledge.
Gilroy, P. 1993. *The Black Atlantic: Modernity and Double Consciousness*. Cambridge, MA: Harvard University Press.
Goldhill, S. 1987. "The Great Dionysia and Civic Ideology." *The Journal of Hellenic Studies* 107: 58–76.
Goldhill, S. 2000. "Civic Ideology and the Problem of Difference: The Politics of Aeschylean Tragedy, Once Again." *The Journal of Hellenic Studies* 120: 34–56.
González, J. M. 2015. "Introduction." Pp. 1–16 in J. M. González ed., *Diachrony: Diachronic Studies of Ancient Greek Literature and Culture*. Berlin/Boston: De Gruyter.
Gowricharn, R. 2009. "Changing Forms of Transnationalism." *Ethnic and Racial Studies* 32 (9): 1619–1638.
Gras, M. 1995. *La Méditerranée archaïque*. Paris: Colin.
Green, P. 1990. *Alexander to Actium: The Historical Evolution of the Hellenistic Age*. Berkeley and Los Angeles: University of California Press.
Güthenke, C. 2009. "Shop Talk: Reception Studies and Recent Work in the History of Scholarship." *Classical Receptions Journal* 1 (1): 104–115.

Hall, E. 1989. *Inventing the Barbarian: Greek Self-Definition through Tragedy.* Oxford: Oxford University Press.
Hall, E. and F. Macintosh. 2005. *Greek Tragedy and the British Theatre 1660–1914.* Oxford: Oxford University Press.
Hallett, J. P. 1993. "Feminist Theory, Historical Periods, Literary Canons, and the Study of Greco-Roman Antiquity." Pp. 54–82 in N. S. Rabinowitz and A. Richlin eds., *Feminist Theory and the Classics.* Abingdon, UK: Routledge.
Hanink, J. 2019. *How to Think about War: An Ancient Guide to Foreign Policy.* Princeton: Princeton University Press.
Hardwick, L. 2003. *Reception Studies.* Cambridge: Cambridge University Press.
Hardwick, L. 2007a. In C. W. Kallendorf ed., *A Companion to the Classical Tradition.* Malden, MA: Wiley-Blackwell.
Hardwick, L. 2007b. In L. Hardwick and C. Gillespie eds., *Classics in Post-Colonial Worlds.* Oxford: Oxford University Press.
Hardwick, L. and C. Stray. 2008. "Introduction: Making Connections." Pp. 1–9 in L. Hardwick and C. Stray eds., *A Companion to Classical Receptions.* Malden, MA: Wiley-Blackwell.
Harris, W. V. ed. 2005. *Rethinking the Mediterranean.* Oxford: Oxford University Press.
Hartog, F. 1988. *The Mirror of Herodotus: The Representation of the Other in the Writing of History.* Berkeley and Los Angeles: University of California Press.
Harvey, D. 1989. *The Condition of Postmodernity an Enquiry into the Origins of Cultural Change.* Cambridge, MA: Blackwell.
Harvey, D. 2009. *Cosmopolitanism and the geographies of freedom.* New York: Columbia University Press.
Haubold, J. 2013. *Greece and Mesopotamia: Dialogues in Literature.* Cambridge: Cambridge University Press.
Hayot, E. 2011. "Against Periodization; or, on Institutional Time." *New Literary History* 42 (4): 739–756.
Held, D., A. McGrew, D. Goldblatt, and J. Perraton. 1999. *Global Transformations: Politics, Economics, Culture.* Stanford, CA: Stanford University Press.
Henderson, J. 2007. "Bringing It All Back Home: Togetherness in Statius's *Silvae* 3.5." *Arethusa* 40: 245–277.
Highet, G. 1949. *The Classical Tradition.* Oxford: Oxford University Press.
Higonnet, M. R. 1994. *Borderwork: Feminist Engagements with Comparative Literature.* Ithaca: Cornell University Press.
Hingley, R. 2005. *Globalizing Roman Culture: Unity, Diversity and Empire.* Abingdon, UK: Routledge.
Hingley, R. 2011. "Globalization and the Roman Empire: The Genealogy of 'Empire'." *Semanta, Ciencias Sociais e Humanidades* 23: 99–113.
Hingley, R. 2015. "Post-Colonial and Global Rome: The Genealogy of Empire." Pp. 32–48 in M. Pitts and J. M. Versluys eds., *Globalization and the Roman World: World History, Connectivity and Material Culture.* Cambridge: Cambridge University Press.
Hitchner, B. 2008. "Globalization avant la lettre: Globalization and the History of the Roman Empire." *New Global Studies* 2: 1–12.

Works cited

Hodos, T. 2006. *Local Responses to Colonization in the Iron Age Mediterranean.* Abingdon, UK: Routledge.
Hodos, T. 2010a. "Local and Global Perspectives in the Study of Social and Cultural Identities." Pp. 3–31 in S. Hales and T. Hodos eds., *Material Culture and Social Identities in the Ancient World.* Cambridge: Cambridge University Press.
Hodos, T. 2010b. "Globalization and Colonization: A View from Iron Age Sicily." *Journal of Mediterranean Archaeology* 23: 81–106.
Hodos, T. 2015. "Global, Local and in between: Connectivity and the Mediterranean." Pp. 240–254 in M. Pitts and J. M. Versluys eds., *Globalization and the Roman World: World History, Connectivity and Material Culture.* Cambridge: Cambridge University Press.
Hodos, T. ed. 2017a. *The Routledge Handbook of Archaeology and Globalization.* Abingdon, UK: Routledge.
Hodos, T. 2017b. "Globalization, Some Basics: An Introduction to *The Routledge Handbook of Archaeology and Globalization.*" Pp. 3–11 in T. Hodos ed., *The Routledge Handbook of Archaeology and Globalization.* Abingdon, UK: Routledge.
Hollis, A. 2011. "Greek Letters from Hellenistic Bactria." Pp. 104–118 in D. Obbink and R. Rutherford eds., *Culture in Pieces: Essays on Ancient Texts in Honour of Peter Parsons.* Oxford: Oxford University Press.
Holmes, B. 2016. "Cosmopoleis in the Field of 'the Classical'." Pp. 269–289 in S. Butler ed., *Deep Classics: Rethinking Classical Reception.* London: Bloomsbury.
Holt, F. L. 1999. *Thundering Zeus: The Making of Hellenistic Bactria.* Berkeley and Los Angeles: University of California Press.
Holt, F. L. 2003. *Alexander the Great and the Mystery of the Elephant Medallions.* Berkeley and Los Angeles: University of California Press.
Holt, F. L. 2012. *Lost World of the Golden King: In Search of Ancient Afghanistan.* Berkeley and Los Angeles: University of California Press.
Holton, R. L. 2011. *Globalization and the Nation State.* Second edition. Basingstoke: Palgrave Macmillan.
Hopkins, A. G. 1999. "Back to the Future: From National History to Imperial History." *Past & Present* 164: 198–243.
Hopkins, A. G. ed. 2002. *Globalisation in World History.* London: Pimlico.
Hopkins, A. G. 2010. "The Historiography of Globalization and the Globalization of Regionalism." *Journal of the Economic and Social History of the Orient* 53: 19–36.
Hopkins, K. 1978. *Conquerors and Slaves.* Cambridge: Cambridge University Press.
Horden, P. and N. Purcell. 2000. *The Corrupting Sea: A Study of Mediterranean History.* Wiley-Blackwell.
Huntington, S. 1996. *The Clash of Civilizations and the Remaking of the World Order.* New York: Simon & Schuster.
Inglis, D. and R. Robertson. 2004. "Beyond the Gates of the Polis: Reworking the Classical Roots of Classical Sociology." *Journal of Classical Sociology* 4 (2): 165–189.
Inglis, D. and R. Robertson. 2005. "The Ecumenical Analytic: 'Globalization', Reflexivity and the Revolution in Greek Historiography." *European Journal of Social Theory* 8 (2): 99–122.

Isayev, E. 2015. "Polybius's Global Moment and Human Mobility through Ancient Italy." Pp. 123–140 in M. Pitts and J. M. Versluys eds., *Globalization and the Roman World: World History, Connectivity and Material Culture*. Cambridge: Cambridge University Press.
Iser, W. 1980. "Interaction between Text and Reader." Pp. 106–119 in S. R. Suleiman and I. Crosman eds., *The Reader in the Text: Essays on Audience and Interpretation*. Princeton: Princeton University Press.
Jauss, H. R. 1970. "Literary History as a Challenge to Literary Theory." *New Literary History* 2 (1): 7–37.
Jennings, J. 2011. *Globalizations and the Ancient World*. Cambridge: Cambridge University Press.
Jennings, J. 2017. "Distinguishing Past Globalizations." Pp. 12–28 in T. Hodos ed., *The Routledge Handbook of Archaeology and Globalization*. Abingdon, UK: Routledge.
Jiménez, A. 2010. "Reproducing Difference: Mimesis and Colonialism in Roman Hispania." Pp. 38–63 in A. B. Knapp and P. van Dommelen eds., *Material Connections in the Ancient Mediterranean: Mobility, Materiality and Mediterranean Identities*. Abingdon, UK: Routledge.
Johns-Putra, A. 2016. "Climate Change in Literature and Literary Studies: From Cli-Fi, Climate Change Theater and Ecopoetry to Ecocriticism and Climate Change Criticism." *Wiley Interdisciplinary Reviews: Climate Change* 7 (2): 266–282.
Kallendorf, C. W. 2007. "Introduction." Pp. 1–4 in C. W. Kallendorf ed., *A Companion to the Classical Tradition*. Malden, MA: Wiley-Blackwell.
Kalliney, P. 2016. *Modernism in a Global Context*. London: Bloomsbury.
Kasimis, D. 2018. *The Perpetual Immigrant and the Limits of Athenian Democracy*. Cambridge: Cambridge University Press.
Kasimis, D. 2020. "Medea the Refugee." *The Review of Politics* 82: 393–415.
Kearney, M. 1995. "The Local and the Global: The Anthropology of Globalization and Transnationalism." *Annual Review of Anthropology* 24: 547–565.
Kendi, I. X. 2016. *Stamped from the Beginning: The Definitive History of Racist Ideas in America*. New York: Nation Books.
Kennedy, George A. 1994. "Shifting Visions of Classical Paradigms: The 'Same' and the 'Other'." *International Journal of the Classical Tradition* 1 (1): 7–16. doi: 10.1007/BF02679075
Kennedy, R. F. 2014. *Immigrant Women in Athens: Gender, Ethnicity, and Citizenship in the Classical City*. Abingdon, UK: Routledge.
Khagram, S. and P. Levitt eds. 2008. *The Transnational Studies Reader: Intersections & Innovations*. Abingdon, UK: Routledge.
Klein, J. T. 2017 [2010]. "Typologies of Interdisciplinarity: The Boundary Work of Definition." Pp. 21–39 in R. Frodeman ed., *The Oxford Handbook of Interdisciplinarity*. Second edition. Oxford: Oxford University Press.
Knapp, A. B. and P. van Dommelen. 2010. "Material Connections: Mobility, Materiality and Mediterranean Identities." Pp. 1–18 in A. B. Knapp and P. van Dommelen eds., *Material Connections in the Ancient Mediterranean: Mobility, Materiality and Mediterranean Identities*. Abingdon, UK: Routledge.
Kosmin, P. J. 2014. *The Land of the Elephant Kings: Space, Territory, and Ideology in the Seleucid Empire*. Cambridge, MA: Harvard University Press.

Works cited

Kosmin, P. J. 2018. *Time and Its Adversaries in the Seleucid Empire*. Cambridge, MA: Harvard University Press.

Kotsonas, A. 2016. "Politics of Periodisation and the Archaeology of Early Greece." *American Journal of Archaeology* 120: 239–270.

Kuhrt, A. and S. Sherwin-White eds. 1987. *Hellenism in the East: The Interaction of Greek and Non-Greek Civilizations from Syria to Central Asia after Alexander*. London: Duckworth.

Lakoff, G. and M. Johnson. 1980. *Metaphors We Live By*. Chicago: University of Chicago Press.

Lakoff, G. and M. Johnson. 1999. *Philosophy in the Flesh: The Embodied Mind and Its Challenge to Western Thought*. New York.

Laurence, R. and F. Trifilò. 2015. "The Global and the Local in the Roman Empire: Connectivity and Mobility from an Urban Perspective." Pp. 99–122 in M. Pitts and J. M. Versluys eds., *Globalization and the Roman World: World History, Connectivity and Material Culture*. Cambridge: Cambridge University Press.

Lefebvre, H. 1991. *The Production of Space*. Translated by Donald Nicholson-Smith. Oxford: Basil Blackwell.

Lerner, J. D. 2003. "The Aï Khanoum Philosophical Papyrus." *Zeitschrift für Papyrologie und Epigraphik* 142: 45–51.

Livingstone, R. W. ed. 1921. *The Legacy of Greece*. Oxford: Oxford University Press.

Loar, M. P., C. MacDonald, and D. Padilla Peralta. 2018. *Rome, Empire of Plunder: The Dynamics of Cultural Appropriation*. Cambridge: Cambridge University Press.

Lowe, L. and D. Lloyd. 1997. *The Politics of Culture in the Shadow of Capital*. Durham, NC: Duke University Press.

Lucas, G. 2005. *The Archaeology of Time*. Abingdon, UK: Routledge.

Mairs, R. 2008. "Greek Identity and the Settler Community in Hellenistic Bactria and Arachosia." *Migrations & Identities* 1 (1): 19–43.

Mairs, R. 2011. *The Archaeology of the Hellenistic Far East: A Survey*. BAR International Series 2196. Oxford: Archaeopress.

Mairs, R. 2013. "The 'Temple with Indented Niches' at Ai Khanoum: Ethnic and Civic Identity in Hellenistic Bactria." Pp. 85–117 in R. Alston, O. M. van Nijf, and C. G. Williamson eds., *Cults, Creeds and Identities in the Greek City after the Classical Age*. Louvain: Peeters.

Mairs, R. 2014. *The Hellenistic Far East: Archaeology, Language and Identity in Greek Central Asia*. Berkeley: University of California Press.

Mairs, R. 2015. "The Founder's Shrine and the Foundation of Ai Khanoum." Pp. 103–128 in N. Mac Sweeney ed., *Foundation Myths in Ancient Societies: Dialogues and Discourses*. Philadelphia: University of Pennsylvania Press.

Malkin, I. ed. 2005. *Mediterranean Paradigms and Classical Antiquity*. Abingdon, UK: Routledge.

Malkin, I. 2011. *A Small Greek World: Networks in the Ancient Mediterranean*. Oxford: Oxford University Press.

Malitz, J. 2000. "Globalisierung? Einheitlichkeit und Vielfalt des Imperium Romanum." Pp. 37–52 in W. Schreiber ed., *Vom Imperium Romanum zum Global Village: "Globalisientngen" im Spiegel der Geschichte*. Neuried: Ars Una.

Marincola, J. 2008. "Universal History from Ephorus to Diodorus." Pp. 155–163 in J. Marincola ed., *A Companion to Greek and Roman Historiography*. Malden, MA: Wiley-Blackwell.
Martindale, C. 1993. *Redeeming the Text: Latin Poetry and the Hermeneutics of Reception*. Cambridge: Cambridge University Press.
Martindale, C. 2007. "Reception." Pp. 297–311 in C. W. Kallendorf ed., *A Companion to the Classical Tradition*. Malden, MA: Wiley-Blackwell.
Martindale, C. 2013. "Reception: A New Humanism? Receptivity, Pedagogy, the Transhistorical." *Classical Receptions Journal* 5 (2): 169–183.
Martinez-Sève, L. 2014. "The Spatial Organization of Ai Khanoum, a Greek City in Afghanistan." *American Journal of Archaeology* 118: 267–283.
Martinez-Sève, L. 2015. "Ai Khanoum and Greek Domination in Central Asia." *Electrum* 22: 17–46.
Mayhew, R. 1995. "Aristotle on the Self-Sufficiency of the City." *History of Political Thought* 16 (4): 488–502.
Mazzarino, S. 1966. *The End of the Ancient World*. Translated by George Holmes. New York: Knopf.
McCarthy, G. E. 2003. *Classical Horizons: The Origins of Sociology in Ancient Greece*. Albany: State University of New York Press.
McCarty, P. 2014. "Globalizing Legal History." *Rechtsgeschichte: Legal History* 22: 283–291.
McClure, J. 2015. "A New Politics of the Middle Ages: A Global Middle Ages for a Global Modernity." *History Compass* 13: 610–619.
McLuhan, M. 1964. *Understanding Media: The Extensions of Man*. London and New York: McGraw-Hill.
McNeill, W. H. 1985. *Polyethnicity and National Unity in World History*. Toronto: University of Toronto Press.
Miller, M. 1997. *Athens and Persia in the Fifth Century B.C.: A Study in Cultural Receptivity*. Cambridge: Cambridge University Press.
Millett, M. 1990. *The Romanization of Britain: An Essay in Archaeological Interpretation*. Cambridge: Cambridge University Press.
Mittelman, J. H. 2005. "What Is a Critical Globalization Studies?" Pp. 19–29 in R. P. Appelbaum and W. I. Robinson eds., *Critical Globalization Studies*. New York: Routledge.
Moloney, E. P. 2015. "Neither Agamemnon Nor Thersites, Achilles Nor Margites: The Heraclid Kings of Ancient Macedon." *Antichthon* 49: 50–72.
Momigliano, A. D. 1966. *Studies in Historiography*. London: Weidenfeld and Nicolson.
Moore, C. 2020. *Calling Philosophers Names: On the Origin of a Discipline*. Princeton: Princeton University Press.
Morley, N. 2015. "Globalisation and the Roman Economy." Pp. 49–68 in M. Pitts and J. M. Versluys eds., *Globalization and the Roman World: World History, Connectivity and Material Culture*. Cambridge: Cambridge University Press.
Morris, I. A. 1999. "The Use and Abuse of Homer." Pp. 52–76 in Irene J. F. DeJong ed., *Homer: Critical Assessments*. Abingdon, UK: Routledge.
Morris, I. A. 2003. "Mediterraneanization." *Mediterranean Historical Review* 18 (2): 30–55.

Moyer, I. 2011. *Egypt and the Limits of Hellenism*. Cambridge: Cambridge University Press.
Müller, C. 2016. "Globalization, Transnationalism, and the Local in Ancient Greece." *Oxford Handbooks Online, Classical Studies, Social and Economic History*. Oxford University Press. [Online].
Murray, G. 1927. *The Classical Tradition in Poetry*. Cambridge, MA: Harvard University Press.
Murray, S. C. 2018. "Lights and Darks: Data, Labeling, and Language in the History of Scholarship on Early Greece." *Hesperia* 87: 17–54.
Mutschler, F.-H. and A. Mittag. 2008. *Conceiving the Empire: China and Rome Compared*. Oxford: Oxford University Press.
Naerebout, F. G. 2006–2007. "Global Romans? Is Globalisation a Concept That Is Going to Help Us Understand the Roman Empire?" *Talanta* 38–9: 149–170.
Nederveen Pieterse, J. 1995. "Globalization as Hybridization." Pp. 45–68 in M. Featherstone, S. Lash, and R. Robertson eds., *Global Modernities*. London: Sage.
Nederveen Pieterse, J. 2013. "What Is Global Studies?" *Globalizations* 10 (4): 499–514.
Nederveen Pieterse, J. 2015. "Ancient Rome and Globalisation: Decentering Rome." Pp. 225–239 in M. Pitts and J. M. Versluys eds., *Globalization and the Roman World: World History, Connectivity and Material Culture*. Cambridge: Cambridge University Press.
Nederveen Pieterse, J. 2017. "Long histories of globalization." Pp. 932–953 in T. Hodos ed., *The Routledge Handbook of Archaeology and Globalization*. Abingdon, UK: Routledge.
Neufeld, M. 1995. *The Restructuring of International Relations Theory*. Cambridge: Cambridge University Press.
Neufeld, M. 2001. "Theorising Globalisation: Towards a Politics of Resistance: A Neo-Gramscian Response to Mathias Albert." *Global Society* 15 (1): 93–106.
Newlands, C. 2002. *Statius' Silvae and the Poetics of Empire*. Cambridge: Cambridge University Press.
Obenga, T. 1995. *A Lost Tradition: African Philosophy in World History*. Philadelphia, PA: Source Editions.
Ober, J. 2006. "Thucydides and the Invention of Political Science." Pp. 131–159 in A. Rengakos and A. Tsakmakis eds., *Brill's Companion to Thucydides*. Leiden: Brill.
Olson, S. D. 2019. "Sophocles in Afghanistan." *The Classical Quarterly* 69 (2): 898–901.
Owen, J. 2015. "Transnationalism as Process, Diaspora as Condition." *Journal of Social Development in Asia* 30 (1): 31–46.
Padilla-Peralta, D. 2019. "Some Thoughts on AIA-SCS 2019." https://medium.com/@danelpadillaperalta/some-thoughts-on-aia-scs-2019-d6a480a1812a. [Online].
Parker, G. 2002. "Ex Oriente Luxuria: Indian Commodities and Roman Experience." *Journal of the Economic and Social History of the Orient* 45 (1): 40–95.
Parmeggiani, G. 2011. *Eforo di Cuma: Studi di storiografia greca*. Bologna: Patron Editore.
Perlman, P. J. 1999 [1998]. "*KRETES AIEI LEISTAI*? The Marginalization of Crete in Greek Thought and the Role of Piracy in the Outbreak of the First Cretan War."

Pp. 110–134 in V. Gabrielsen ed., *Hellenistic Rhodes: Politics, Culture and Society*. Aarhus: Aarhus Universitetsforlag.

Petzold, M., J. Rüpke, and C. Steimle. 2001. "Römische Reichsreligion und Provinzialreligion: Globalisierungs- und Regionalisierungsprozesse in der antiken Religionsgeschichte." *Archiv Für Religionsgeschichte* 3: 296–307.

Pitts, M. 2015. "Globalisation, Circulation and Mass Consumption in the Roman World." Pp. 69–98 in M. Pitts and J. M. Versluys eds., *Globalization and the Roman World: World History, Connectivity and Material Culture*. Cambridge: Cambridge University Press.

Pitts, M. and J. M. Versluys. 2015a. "Introduction." Pp. 3–31 in M. Pitts and J. M. Versluys eds., *Globalization and the Roman World: World History, Connectivity and Material Culture*. Cambridge: Cambridge University Press.

Pitts, M. and J. M. Versluys eds. 2015b. *Globalization and the Roman World: World History, Connectivity and Material Culture*. Cambridge: Cambridge University Press.

Pogorzelski, R. 2016. "Centers and Peripheries." Pp. 223–238 in A. Zissos ed., *A Companion to the Flavian Age of Imperial Rome*. Malden, MA: Wiley-Blackwell.

Pollock, S. 1995. "Literary History, Indian History, World History." *Social Scientist* 23 (10/12): 112–142.

Pomeroy, A. J. 2003. "Center and Periphery in Tacitus' *Histories*." *Arethusa* 36: 361–374.

Porter, J. I. 2008. "Reception Studies: Future Prospects." Pp. 469–481 in L. Hardwick and C. Stray eds., *A Companion to Classical Receptions*. Malden, MA: Wiley-Blackwell.

Rankine, P. D. 2019. "The Classics, Race, and Community-Engaged or Public Scholarship." *American Journal of Philology* 140: 345–359.

Rapin, C. I. 1990. "Greeks in Afghanistan: Ai Khanum." Pp. 329–342 in J.-P. Descœudres ed., *Greek Colonists and Native Populations*. Oxford: Oxford University Press.

Rapin, C. I. 1996. "Nouvelles observations sur le parchemin gréco-bactrien d'Asangôrna." *Topoi* 6 (2): 458–469.

Rapin, C. and F. Grenet. 1983. "Inscriptions économiques de la trésorerie hellénistique d'Aï Khanoum. L'onomastique iranienne à Aï Khanoum." *Bulletin de correspondance hellénique* 107 (1): 315–381.

Rapin, C. I., P. Hadot Pierre, and G. Cavallo. 1987. "Les textes littéraires grecs de la Trésorerie d'Aï Khanoum." *Bulletin de correspondance hellénique* 111 (1): 225–266.

Rawlings, H. R. 2015. "Why We Need to Read Thucydides: Even When 'We' Are Only a Few." Pp. 551–559 in Christine Lee ed., *A Handbook to the Reception of Thucydides*. Malden, MA: Wiley-Blackwell.

Rehm, R. 1989. "Aeschylus in Syracuse: The Commerce of Tragedy and Politics" Pp. 31–34 in B. Daix Westcoat ed., *Syracuse, the Fairest Greek City*. Rome: De Luca Edizioni D'Arte.

Rhodes. P. J. 2003. "Nothing to Do with Democracy: Athenian Drama and the Polis." *The Journal of Hellenic Studies* 123: 104–119.

Rivas Sacconi, José Manuel. 1993 [1949]. *El Latín en Colombia*. Bogotá: Inst. Caro y Cuervo.

Robb, J. 2007. *The Early Mediterranean Village: Agency, Material Culture, and Social Change in Neolithic Italy*. Cambridge: Cambridge University Press.

Works cited

Robertson, R. 1992. *Globalization: Social Theory and Global Culture*. London: Sage.
Robertson, R. 1995. "Glocalization: Time-Space and Homogeneity-Heterogeneity." Pp. 25–44 in M. Featherstone, S. Lash, and R. Robertson eds., *Global Modernities*. London: Sage.
Robinson, W. I. 2005. "What Is a Critical Globalization Studies? Intellectual Labor and Global Society." Pp. 11–18 in R. P. Appelbaum and W. I. Robinson eds., *Critical Globalization Studies*. New York: Routledge.
Rouse, R. 1991. "Mexican Migration and the Social Space of Postmodernism." *Diaspora* 1 (1): 8–23.
Rouse, R. 1995. "Questions of Identity: Personhood and Collectivity in Transnational Migration to the United States." *Critique of Anthropology* 15 (4): 351–380.
Rowlands, M. 1987. "Centre and Periphery: A Review of the Concept." Pp. 1–11 in M. Rowlands, M. Larsen, and K. Kristiansen eds., *Centre and Periphery in the Ancient World*. Cambridge: Cambridge University Press.
Rowlands, M. 2010. "Concluding Thoughts." Pp. 233–247 in A. B. Knapp and P. van Dommelen eds., *Material Connections in the Ancient Mediterranean: Mobility, Materiality and Mediterranean Identities*. Abingdon, UK: Routledge.
Sadowski-Smith, C. ed. 2002. *Globalization on the Line: Culture, Capital, and Citizenship at U.S. Borders*. New York: Palgrave.
Salter, W. H. 1911. *Essay on Two Moderns: Euripides, Samuel Butler*. London: Sidgwick & Jackson.
Santos, Boaventura de Sousa. 2004. "A Critique of Lazy Reason: Against the Waste of Experience." Pp. 157–197 in Immanuel Wallerstein ed., *The Modern World-System in the Longue Durée*. London: Paradigm.
Saussure, F. de. 1971. *Cours de linguistique générale*. Paris: Payot.
Schäfer, W. 2007. "Global History." Pp. 516–521 in Jan Aart Scholte and Roland Robertson eds., *Encyclopedia of Globalization*. 4 volumes. Abingdon, UK: Routledge.
Scheidel, W. ed. 2009. *Rome and China: Comparative Perspectives on Ancient World Empires*. Oxford: Oxford University Press.
Schein, S. 2008. "'Our Debt to Greece and Rome': Canon, Class and Ideology." Pp. 75–85 in L. Hardwick and C. Stray eds., *A Companion to Classical Receptions*. Malden, MA: Wiley-Blackwell.
Segal, C. P. 1995. "Classis, Ecumenicism, and Greek Tragedy." *Transactions of the American Philological Association* 125: 1–26.
Seo, J. M. 2019. "Classics for All: Future Antiquity from a Global Perspective." *American Journal of Philology* 140 (4): 699–715.
Sfameni Gasparro, G. 2004–2005. "Globalizzazione e localizzazione della religione dall'Ellenismo al Tardo Antico." *Koinonia* 28–9: 81–104.
Shanks, M. and C. Tilly. 1987. *Social Theory and Archaeology*. Albuquerque, NM: University of New Mexico Press.
Shaw, B. 2001. "Challenging Braudel: A New Vision of the Mediterranean." *Journal of Roman Archaeology* 14: 419–453.
Shumate, N. 2006. *Nation, Empire, Decline: Studies in Rhetorical Continuity from the Romans to the Modern Era*. London: Duckworth.
Sick, D. H. 2007. "When Socrates Met the Buddha: Greek and Indian Dialectic in Hellenistic Bactria and India." *Journal of the Royal Asiatic Society* 17 (3): 253–278.

Silk, M., I. Gildenhard, and R. Barrow. 2014. *The Classical Tradition: Art, Literature, Thought*. Malden, MA: Wiley-Blackwell.

Sklair, L. 2005. "Generic Globalization, Capitalist Globalization, and Beyond: A Framework for Critical Globalization Studies." Pp. 55–63 in R. P. Appelbaum and W. I. Robinson eds., *Critical Globalization Studies*. New York: Routledge.

Smith, D. E. 1977. *Feminism and Marxism: A Place to Begin: A Way to Go*. Vancouver: New Star.

Snodgrass, A. M. 1974. "An Historical Homeric Society?" *Journal of Hellenic Studies* 94: 114–125.

Snodgrass, A. M. 2000 [1971]. *The Dark Age of Greece*. Reissue. Edinburgh: University Press.

Snodgrass, A. M. 2015. "Diachrony in Greek Agriculture." Pp. 347–362 in J. González ed., *Diachrony Diachronic Studies of Ancient Greek Literature and Culture*. Berlin/Boston: De Gruyter.

Soja, E. W. 1996. *Thirdspace: Journeys to Los Angeles and Other Real-and-Imagined Places*. Cambridge, MA: Blackwell.

Sommer, M. 2015. "OIKOYMENH: longue duree Perspectives on Ancient Mediterranean 'Globality'." Pp. 175–197 in M. Pitts and J. M. Versluys eds., *Globalization and the Roman World: World History, Connectivity and Material Culture*. Cambridge: Cambridge University Press.

Spawforth, A. 2018. *The Story of Greece and Rome*. New Haven, CT: Yale University Press.

Spier, F. 2015. *Big History and the Future of Humanity*. Malden, MA: Wiley-Blackwell.

Spivak, G. C. 2003. *Death of a Discipline*. New York: Columbia University Press.

Stearns, P. N. 2010. *Globalization in World History*. Abingdon, UK: Routledge.

Steger, M. B. 2008. *The Rise of the Global Imaginary: Political Ideologies from the French Revolution to the Global War on Terror*. Oxford: Oxford University Press.

Steger, M. B. 2017. *Globalization: A Very Short Introduction*. Oxford: Oxford University Press.

Steger, M. and A. Wahlrab. 2017. *What Is Global Studies?* Abingdon, UK: Routledge.

Stewart, E. 2017. *Greek Tragedy on the Move: The Birth of a Panhellenic Art Form c.500–300 BC*. Oxford: Oxford University Press.

Stoll, O. 2007. "The Religions of the Armies." Pp. 451–476 in P. Erdkamp ed., *A Companion to the Roman Army*. Malden, MA: Wiley-Blackwell.

Strauss, D. 2006. *The Trojan War: A New History*. New York: Simon & Schuster.

Stray, C. 2007. "Education." Pp. 5–14 in C. W. Kallendorf ed., *A Companion to the Classical Tradition*. Malden, MA: Wiley-Blackwell.

Sweetman, R. J. 2007. "Roman Knossos: The Nature of a Globalized City." *American Journal of Archaeology* 111 (1): 61–81.

Tarn, W. W. 1938. *The Greeks in Bactria and India*. Cambridge: Cambridge University Press.

Taylor, C. and K. Vlassopoulos. 2015. "Introduction: An Agenda for the Study of Greek History." Pp. 1–31 in C. Taylor and K. Vlassopoulos eds., *Communities and Networks in the Ancient Greek World*. Oxford: Oxford University Press.

Tomlinson, J. 1999. *Globalization and Culture*. Chicago: University of Chicago Press.

van Dommelen, P. 2012. "Colonialism and Migration in the Ancient Mediterranean." *Annual Review of Anthropology* 41: 393–409.
van Dommelen, P. and A. B. Knapp eds. 2010. Material Connections in the Ancient Mediterranean. Mobility, Materiality and Mediterranean Identities. Abington, UK: Routledge.
Vasunia, P. 2001. *The Gift of the Nile: Hellenizing Egypt from Aeschylus to Alexander*. Berkeley: University of California Press.
Vasunia, P. 2005. "(C.) Dougherty and (L.) Kurke Eds. The Cultures within Ancient Greek Culture. Contact, Conflict, Collaboration. Cambridge UP, 2003. Pp. xx + 289, illus. £50/$70. 0521815665.—(J.) Siapkas Heterological Ethnicity. Conceptualizing Identities in Ancient Greece. (Acta Universitatis Upsaliensis. Boreas: Uppsala Studies in Ancient Mediterranean and Near Eastern Civilizations, 27). Uppsala, 2003. Pp. x + 333, 1 table, 1 map. Sw. kr. 230. 9155458238." *The Journal of Hellenic Studies* 125: 178–180.
Vasunia, P. 2011. "The Comparative Study of Empires." *The Journal of Roman Studies* 101: 222–237.
Versluys, M. J. 2015. "Roman Visual Material Culture as Globalising *koine*." Pp. 141–174 in M. Pitts and J. M. Versluys eds., *Globalization and the Roman World: World History, Connectivity and Material Culture*. Cambridge: Cambridge University Press.
Vertovec, S. 1999. "Conceiving and Researching Transnationalism." *Ethnic and Racial Studies* 22 (2): 447–462.
Vertovec, S. 2001. "Transnationalism and Identity." *Journal of Ethnic and Migration Studies* 27 (4): 573–582.
Vickers, J. 1997. "'[U]framed in Open, Unmapped Fields': Teaching and the Practice of Interdisciplinarity." *Arachnē: An Interdisciplinary Journal of the Humanities* 4 (2): 11–42.
Vlassopoulos, K. 2007. *Unthinking the Greek Polis: Ancient Greek History beyond Eurocentrism*. Cambridge: Cambridge University Press.
Vlassopoulos, K. 2013. *Greeks and Barbarians*. Cambridge: Cambridge University Press.
Wachsmuth, C. and O. Hense. 1884–1894. *Ioannis Stobaei Anthologium*. 3 volumes. Berlin: Weidmann.
Walbank, F. W. 1957–1979. *A Historical Commentary on Polybius*. 3 volumes. Oxford: Oxford University Press.
Walbank, F. W. 2002. *Polybius, Rome and the Hellenistic World: Essays and Reflections*. Cambridge: Cambridge University Press.
Wallace, S. 2016. "Greek Culture in Afghanistan and India: Old Evidence and New Discoveries." *Greece & Rome* 63 (2): 205–226.
Wallerstein, I. 1974a. "The Rise and Future Demise of the World Capitalist System: Concepts for Comparative Analysis." *Comparative Studies in Society and History* 16 (4): 387–415.
Wallerstein, I. 1974b. *The Modern World System: Capitalist Agriculture and the Origins of the European World-Economy in the Sixteenth Century*. New York: Academic Press.
Wallerstein, I. 1980. *The Modern World System II: Mercantilism and the Consolidation of the European World-Economy, 1600–1750*. New York: Academic Press.

Walton, J. M. 2009. *Euripides Our Contemporary*. London: Methuen Drama.
Waters, M. 1995. *Globalization*. Second edition. Abingdon, UK: Routledge.
Whitmarsh, T. 2010. "Thinking Local." Pp. 1–16 in T. Whitmarsh ed., *Local Knowledge and Microidentities in the Imperial Greek World*. Cambridge: Cambridge University Press.
Wijma, S. M. 2014. *Embracing the Immigrant: The Participation of Metics in Athenian Polis Religion (5th–4th Century BC)*. Stuttgart: Franz Steiner.
Wilkinson, D. 1993. "Civilizations, Cores, World Economies, and Oikoumenes." Pp. 221–246 in A. G. Frank and B. K. Gills eds., *The World System: Five Hundred Years or Five Thousand?* Abingdon, UK: Routledge.
Wilson, M. 1993. "Flavian Variant: History: Silius' *Punica*." Pp. 218–236 in A. J. Boyle ed., *Roman Epic*. Abingdon, UK: Routledge.
Wilson, P. 2011. "The Glue of Democracy? Tragedy, Structure, and Finance." Pp. 19–44 in D. M. Carter ed., *Why Athens? A Reappraisal of Tragic Politics*. Oxford: Cambridge University Press.
Witcher, R. 2000. "Globalisation and Roman Imperialism: Perspectives on Identities in Roman Italy." Pp. 213–225 in E. Herring and K. Lomas eds., *The Emergence of State Identities in Italy in the First Millennium BC*. London: Accordia.
Witcher, R. 2017. "The Globalized Roman World." Pp. 634–651 in T. Hodos ed., *The Routledge Handbook of Archaeology and Globalization*. Abingdon, UK: Routledge.
Wolf, E. 1982. *Europe and the People without History*. Berkeley and Los Angeles: University of California Press.
Woolf, G. 1997. "Beyond Romans and Natives." *World Archaeology* 28: 339–350.
Woolf, G. 1998. *Becoming Roman: The Origins of Provincial Civilization in Gaul*. Cambridge: Cambridge University Press.
Woolf, G. 2005. "A Sea of Faith?" Pp. 126–143 in I. Malkin ed., *Mediterranean Paradigms and Classical Antiquity*. Abingdon, UK: Routledge.
Yailenko, V.-P. 1990. "Les maximes Delphiques d'Aï Khanoum et la formation de la doctrine du dhamma d'Asoka." *Dialogues d'histoire ancienne* 16: 239–256.
Zajko, V. 2008. "'What Difference Was Made?': Feminist Models of Reception." Pp. 195–206 in L. Hardwick and C. Stray eds., *A Companion to Classical Receptions*. Malden, MA: Wiley-Blackwell.
Zanker, A. T. 2019. *Metaphor in Homer: Time, Speech, and Thought*. Cambridge: Cambridge University Press.
Zinkina, J. et al. 2019. *A Big History of Globalization: The Emergence of a Global World System*. Cham, Switzerland: Springer.
Ziolkowski, J. M. 2007. "Middle Ages." Pp. 17–29 in C. W. Kallendorf ed., *A Companion to the Classical Tradition*. Malden, MA: Wiley-Blackwell.
Zuckerberg, D. 2018. *Not All Dead White Men*. Cambridge, MA: Harvard University Press.

Index

Afghanistan *see* Ai Khanoum
Ai Khanoum 16, 26, 33–41
Alexander the Great 26–27, 29–31, 35–36, 38, 40, 42
alienation 13, 53, 72, 75n21, 93
Amin, Samir 20–21
anthropology 56–57, 60, 63–64, 83–84
antiquity 1–2, 6–13, 102–104;
  globalization in 17–26; multiple 71–75;
  transborder 16, 31, 34–35, 41–43;
  transdisciplinary 78–80, 83–88, 92–96;
  transhistorical 49, 54, 60–67, 70
Apollonius of Rhodes 37, 84
Appelbaum, Richard 89–90, 95
archaeology 7–10, 12–14; transborder 21–22, 24–25, 34–37, 40, 42;
  transdisciplinary 83, 86; transhistorical 50–52, 54–55, 57, 59–60
Arendt, Hannah 53
Aristotle 26–27
Asoka 35, 37–38

Barber, Benjamin 34, 43
Barrow, Rosemary 66, 69
Beecroft, Alexander 42–43
Bernal, Martin 20
border studies 17
bottom-up constructions 34, 93
Bourdieu, Pierre 88–90
Braudel, Fernand 19, 23, 60
Buddhism 35, 37–38

chronology 18, 21, 38, 50, 53–55, 57
civilization 7–8, 20–21, 43–44, 55–57, 85–87

classical studies 6, 10, 102; transborder 23, 41; transdisciplinary 83–88, 95;
  transhistorical 54, 62, 70
collaboration 5–6, 14, 16, 82, 84, 96, 104
colonization 29, 57, 72, 76n39
comparative study 9–10, 24, 42–43, 49, 71, 79, 92–93
consumption 33, 91
continuity and discontinuity 13;
  transborder 30; transdisciplinary 78, 93; transhistorical 56, 59–61, 65, 71–74
critical reflexivity 91–92, 98
critical theory 62, 66, 85
cultural aggregation 103
cultural flows 44, 71, 102

Davies, J. K. 59–60
decentering 9–10, 16–18, 41–42, 60, 70, 84, 91, 104
decolonization 8, 54, 66, 78
deterritorializing 41, 54, 99
dhamma 37–38
diaspora 17, 29
Doniger, Wendy 43
Dozier, Curtis 96

ecumenical, the: in Polybius 26–33
ecumenicism 79–88
Eliot, T. S. 62–63
Ephorus 27–28, 30–41, 46n64
essentialism 11, 103
ethics: of addressing contemporary global issues through classics 1; of consumption 33; critical 75, 94–95;

of government 26; Greek ethical philosophies 38; of periodization and chronology 54; of preservation and transmission 67; of representation 103; of scholars and academics 89–90
Euripides 62–63, 69, 84
Eurocentrism 5, 7, 9, 14, 87; transborder 20–21, 39–42; transhistorical 54–55, 68–69, 72, 74
exploitation 33, 82

Fabian, Johannes 56–58, 72
Farrell, Joseph 10, 84–87, 92
feminism 67–68, 71, 74, 84–85, 94
Ferguson, Marjorie 33
Flynn, D. O. 18–19, 57

generalization 40–41, 44, 85, 102–103
George, Susan 90–91, 94
Giddens, Anthony 2, 19
Gildenhard, Ingo 66, 69
Gilroy, Paul 20, 42
Giráldez, A. 18–19, 57
global, the 5, 13; in antiquity 17–26; in Polybius 26–33; transborder 34, 41, 43; transdisciplinary 79–88; transhistorical 49–50, 69, 71, 75; *see also* glocalization
globalization 1–2, 102–104; and global classics 6–12; and global studies 2–6; transborder 16–23, 25–29, 31–34, 39, 41–44; transdisciplinary 78–80, 83–84, 87–91, 93–95, 97–99; transhistorical 49–54, 56–57, 60–62, 67, 71–75
global studies 1–6, 9–14, 102–104; transborder 16–17; transdisciplinary 78–80, 83–84, 88–89, 94–95, 98–99; transhistorical 50–52, 75
global turn 10, 12–14, 78–79, 84, 88
glocalization 13, 25, 42–43, 52; at Ai Khanoum 33–41
government 21, 26, 54, 89

Hanink, Johana 96–97
Hardwick, Lorna 67
Harvey, David 18, 53–54
Hayot, Eric 54, 85

Hellenization 27, 29, 40–41, 68; Panhellenization 42
Hesiod 56
Hingley, Richard 25
Hitchner, Bruce 25
holism 9, 66, 79–88, 92, 95, 97, 104
Homer 32, 37, 56–58, 62–63, 84
homogenization 2, 4, 88, 103; transborder 24, 33–34, 41–44; transhistorical 55, 71, 73–74
Hopkins, A. G. 5, 19–20
Horden, Peregrine 9, 23, 51–52

imaginaries 6, 14, 18, 68–69
Inglis, David 27
international 4–6, 13, 17, 42, 68
intersectionality 94
Isocrates 27, 30, 46n65

Kallendorf, Craig 66, 68–69
Kennedy, George 68–69

Lefebvre, Henri 52, 54
local, the 1–3, 11, 13, 21–26, 41–44, 84, 91–95; *see also* glocalization
longue durée 5, 31, 53, 60–61, 99
Lysippus 39

Malkin, Irad 23–24
marginalization and marginalized viewpoints and groups 21, 42, 56–58, 74, 92, 96–98, 103
Martial 21
Marxism 19–20, 66, 68
McLuhan, Marshall 53, 75n21
Mediterraneanism, new 9, 34
Middle Ages 19, 56, 72, 86
Mittelman, James 90–91, 93–94
modernity 11; transborder 18–20, 41; transdisciplinary 86, 88, 97, 99; transhistorical 55–56, 60, 62, 71–74
Momigliano, Arnaldo 51–52
Morris, Ian 23
Murray, Gilbert 63–64
Murray, Sarah 55, 76n29
myth 33–34, 43

Naerebout, F. G. 25
Neufeld, Mark 94–95

occidentalism 5, 7–9, 14, 20, 40, 72–73, 93–94
Ovid 21, 84

Panhellenism 21, 24, 27–30, 39, 42, 84, 91
pedagogy 13–14, 80, 92
periodization 11, 13, 20, 49–50, 54–61, 71–74, 85; antiperiodizing 99
PHAROS 96
place 50–53, 79, 85, 98; and periodization 54–61
Plato 26–27, 69, 92
politics 2–3; of representation 103; transborder 19, 22–31, 33–34, 42–44; transdisciplinary 81–82, 89–91, 97–99; transhistorical 53–55, 57–58, 60, 73–74
Pollock, Sheldon 43–44
Polybius 16, 26–33, 40–41, 46n64
Porter, James 92–93, 97
postcolonialism 20, 42, 66–68, 71–72, 74
postmodernism 18, 24, 71, 73, 102
presentism 14, 20, 53
preservation 64, 67
Purcell, Nicholas 9, 23, 51–52

reception: transdisciplinary 83, 88, 93, 97; transhistorical 56, 62, 66–71, 73–74
regional 16, 20–21, 26–27, 29, 32–31, 43–44
religious culture and practices 36–39
representation 66, 82, 103
research design 14, 94, 99
Robertson, Roland 27, 34, 52
Robinson, William 89–91
Romanization 23, 25, 29, 32–33

Salter, W. H. 62–63
Saussure, Ferdinand de 58–59
scale 25–27, 33–34, 60, 102–103
scope 20, 102, 103
Second World War 65–66
Sick, David 37–38

Silius Italicus 21
Silk, Michael 66, 69
Snodgrass, A. M. 56–57, 59, 76n29
social consciousness 3, 13, 25–26, 29, 52, 91
social well-being 14, 78–79, 104
Socrates 26, 92, 100n8
Soja, Edward 24, 52
space and time 50–53, 79, 85; and periodization 54–61
Statius 21
superregional 41

Tacitus 21
Thucydides 27, 65–66, 96–97
time *see* space and time
top-down view 11, 34, 43, 93, 98, 103
tradition 10–11, 62–71, 73–74
transborder 13, 16, 41–44, 83–84, 88, 104; global and ecumenical in Polybius 26–33; glocalization at Ai Khanoum 33–41; globalization in antiquity 17–26
transdisciplinary 5–7, 12–14, 51, 78–79, 98–99, 104; and critical global classics 88–98; holism, ecumenicism, and the global 79–88
transgressive 104
transhistorical 7, 13, 49–50, 102, 104; multiple antiquities 71–75; time and place 50–61; tradition, reception, and beyond 61–71; and the transborder 33, 44; and the transdisciplinary 78–79, 84, 87–88, 91–93, 97–99
transmission 64, 66–67
transnational 2–3, 13, 17–18, 41–43

Vasunia, Phiroze 22, 92–93
Vlassopoulos, K. 24, 30, 34, 55

Wallerstein, Immanuel 19–22

Zola, Émile 89

For Product Safety Concerns and Information please contact our EU representative GPSR@taylorandfrancis.com
Taylor & Francis Verlag GmbH, Kaufingerstraße 24, 80331 München, Germany